Grip Strength

How to close heavy duty hand grippers, lift thick bar weights, and pinch grip just about anything

Paperback edition

Robert Spindler
with Tommy Heslep

© 2013. All rights reserved. No part of this book may be reproduced or transmitted in any form or by any means without written permission.

ISBN-13: 978-1492734000
ISBN-10: 1492734004

ACKNOWLEDGEMENTS

Robert would like to thank his parents.

Tommy would like to thank:

God, first and foremost, for giving him the ability to do all he did and does.

Definitely his wife, Mary Jo, as she put up with quite a bit over the past seven years.

His dad, who passed some good genes on to Tommy, still having huge forearms on him.

John Brookfield and Dennis Rogers for their inspiration.

DISCLAIMER

The information in this book is to be used at your own risk and is no replacement for professional health care advice. We strongly advise you to consult a physician prior to beginning a physical training program. If you experience any discomfort or pain performing the exercises described in this book or following the advice given in it, interrupt your training immediately and seek qualified advice.

Furthermore, the authors encourage you to refrain from the use of performance-enhancing drugs.

ABOUT THE AUTHORS

Robert Spindler is a professional stage strongman and two-time Austrian powerlifting champion. Read more about him at:
www.Eisen-Hans.at

Tommy Heslep is world-renowned grip strength expert and world-record holder. Read more about him in chapter two, "About Tommy Heslep".

CONTENTS

1. About this Book	9
2. About Tommy Heslep	11
3. Getting Started	17
3.1. The Different Types of Grip Strength	17
Summary	20
3.2. Location	21
Summary	23
3.3. Tools	24
3.3.1. Advanced Tools	29
3.3.2. Tools for Recovery	34
Summary	37
3.4. Warm-Up	38
Summary	41
3.5. Frequency	42
Summary	44
4. Crushing Grip: Closing Heavy-Duty Grippers	45
4.1. The Captains of Crush® Grippers	45
Summary	51
4.2. How to Hold a Gripper Correctly	52
Summary	58
4.3. Training with Grippers: Exercises	59
Summary	67
4.4. Training with Grippers: Reps and Sets	68
Summary	71
5. Pinch Grip	73
5.1. Pinch Grip: Exercises	74
Summary	86

6. Thick Bar Training	87
Summary	94
7. Endurance Grip Strength	99
Summary	104
8. Additional Training	105
Summary	116
9. Sample Training Routines	117
10. Grip Strength Feats	129
Summary	139
11. Recovery, Plateaus, and Injury Prevention	141
11.1. Recovery	141
11.2. Plateaus	148
11.3. Injury Prevention	150
Summary	154
12. Nutrition	155
Summary	157
13. Common Mistakes	159
Summary	165
14. Afterword	167
Recommended Books and DVDs	169

1. ABOUT THIS BOOK

This book is about grip strength. First and foremost, it focuses on the crushing grip, the kind of strength you need to close heavy duty hand grippers. It also has a section on the pinch grip, one on thick bar training, one on endurance grip strength and one on several grip strength feats you might want to try, including lifting the Dinnie Stones. (This book does not cover wrist strength or wrist strength feats.) As you will see, it covers training for any kind of strength that is classified as grip strength by the most universally accepted definition.

This book is the result of several interviews I did with Tommy Heslep. Tommy has two of the strongest hands in the world. This book is a portrait of this charismatic grip strength athlete, as well as a summary of the training methods which enabled him to achieve some of his amazing feats.

In writing this book we aimed for simplicity. We tried to present the facts so they can be put to use right away. I will give you sources for more detailed information and theory along the way.

This book does not claim to be the sole authority on grip strength training. It describes what worked for Tommy Heslep. And although I believe that his methods will work for most if applied correctly, they are neither the *only* way that works, nor will they work for *everybody* the same way they did for Tommy. We are too sensible to make a claim like that.

One aim of this book is to demonstrate that Tommy is a man like you and me. He is neither a genetic freak, nor did he do anything utterly unusual to reach his goals. He also paid his dues and made mistakes. We will cover all of that here. We want you to learn from his experiences so you won't make the same mistakes. If there is anything that sets Tommy apart, it is his attitude and willpower, and that is something you can't teach. But apart from that you can do anything Tommy did, and if you do, we're confident that you will build a monster grip as well.

This book is for anyone who wants to bring his grip strength to a new level - whether you are rock climber, powerlifter, Traceur, wrestler, judoka, gymnast, MMA fighter, strongman, or just want to impress your friends by crushing an apple in one hand. You will benefit from the advice in this book. Even if it just helps you to avoid injuries resulting from imbalanced training. Primarily, this book is aimed at those who have become intrigued by heavy-duty hand grippers like the IronMind® Captains of Crush®. We still believe that they are amongst the most effective ways to strengthen your grip - for whatever aim – if you do it right.

And now, learn about the man who is amongst the very few (they are only five at the time I'm writing this) who ever got certified for closing the dreaded #4 Captains of Crush® Gripper, and learn how he got there.

2. ABOUT TOMMY HESLEP

Tommy Heslep, born in 1974, has easily one of the strongest grips in the world. Some of his grip strength feats include: **pinch lifting two 45 lbs plates** with only thumb, index, and middle finger, **keeping two aeroplanes from taking off** only with the strength of his two hands for over a minute, and with **only one hand** for almost a minute, **crushing twelve raw potatoes in a row** with one hand, a **no-set close of the #3** CoC® in either hand, **bending the IronMind® Red Nail**, and certifying for **closing the #4 CoC®**.

How did he do all of this?

I can give you the answer right away: with industry, perseverance, and faith. This is basically Tommy's secret.

If this is all, you might ask, why this book? Well, this book is meant to supply all the know-how, anything you will need apart from these features, to build a monster grip. But still you will not get anywhere if you lack the industry to give every training session your all, the perseverance to train your grip regularly over the years it takes to reach your goals, or the faith that you will reach said goals. So bear the importance of this in mind.

Back to Tommy.

It all started in '93, when he saw an advertisement for the Ivanko Super Gripper in a muscle magazine. There was a picture of a guy with a huge forearm beside it and that was what Tommy wanted. He had already teamed up with a couple of friends, regularly training the "mirror muscles", as he calls them. But he didn't even know grip strength existed at the time - all he wanted were the bigger forearms. He purchased the gripper and worked on it hard. It would take him some time to learn that there is something better even than looking strong, which is actually *being* strong. But without Tommy knowing, the Ivanko Super Gripper steered him towards that goal and definitely helped as a foundation for some of his later achievements.

In '94 Tommy became a Christian. While watching a Christian programming on TV, he got his first glimpse of Oldtime Strongman feats. A group of big guys toured schools and churches around the country, ripping phone books, bending steel bars, and the like. Tommy was impressed and eager to try the same, but at the time didn't know how to get into this exotic sport. A year passed, and in '95 he heard on the radio that another strongman would perform live at a church only an hour's drive away from where Tommy was living at the time. This time he decided to be there. He went there with a few friends, expecting a huge guy on stage just like the ones he had seen on TV.

The performing strongman was bald, about 150 pounds, and small. It was Dennis Rogers, probably the most famous steel-bender alive. Seeing Dennis perform live blew Tommy away. He couldn't believe someone that small could be that strong. Dennis was bending wrenches, ripping huge phone books, tearing decks of cards, and bending steel nails. He let Tommy try one of the phone books, but Tommy couldn't do anything with it. But he got a chance to walk up to the man after the show for a chat. "How come you can do all this stuff I can't?" Tommy asked. "It's all tendon strength, from the tendons. Start small and keep at it," Rogers replied.

That's a dangerous thing to say to someone as determined as Tommy, who eventually kept at it until he reached world class. Having learned that looks and size are deceiving when it comes to strength, he went right home, grabbed the first spike he could find – a 40-penny nail –, wrapped a bandage around the ends and went at it. After 10 or 15 minutes, the thing was U-shaped. But he needed more proof. He shuffled through all the drawers in his house until a deck of cards got into his hands. After 20 minutes of tearing and wearing, the thing finally gave in as well. He didn't stop until he ripped them. Perhaps he should have, but he didn't.

Tommy paid with two big bubble blisters on his thumb pads which were there for a week. But he was happy: finally, he knew what he was supposed to do.

And he did it exceptionally well. In 2010 he broke the world record of keeping two planes from taking off with grip strength only. He put them on hold for about 1min 15sec, where his precursor held them for just over a minute, with wraps around his arms – using the whole of his upper body (the classic "human link" feat of strength). Tommy held them simply by two steel triangles, similar to holding a Captains of Crush® Gripper closed, using his grip strength only. The aeroplanes he was holding back were even using more horsepower than those of his precursor. It was 815 pounds of pressure on his body altogether. "It was pretty tough," Tommy told me.

Fig. 2.1 Tommy getting ready to hold back two aeroplanes with bare hands

In 2011 he did a similar stunt, using one hand only (!) to prevent the two aeroplanes from taking off. He didn't aim for a record with that one, but held them back for almost a minute as well.

This man, who had a "probably average grip" before he started out, is most well-known in the world of grip strength today for being one of the few lucky ones to have certified for closing the IronMind® #4 Captains of Crush® Gripper. His road to this achievement was a long and winded one, though. Remember that he started training his grip with the Ivanko gripper in 1993, but wasn't certified for the #4 until 2004. That's 11 years of endless workouts for one specific goal. 11 years! That's what I call willpower. So much for anyone who gives up on the grippers after a few months of training because his progress stagnates.

But let's go over Tommy's road to success step by step. Like mentioned, he had been training with the Ivanko gripper (probably with not much of a regime) until he could close it on the highest setting (it has springs which can be adjusted to increase the resistance). He had heard somewhere that this would be similar in difficulty to closing a #3 Captains of Crush® Gripper, which he eventually purchased in 1998 to give it a try. He took it out of the zip bag they came in back then, and realized that it was too big for his hand. He used his left hand to close it with both hands in front of his chest just enough to get his pinky finger of the right hand around it. Then he stuck his right arm out and tried to close it. He got it down to about three quarters of an inch to half an inch space left between the handles.

Of course, being an optimist, Tommy had thought he could close the #3 the first time he tried – having closed the Ivanko gripper at the highest setting before –, and was disillusioned in this respect. But at least there was a new challenge. Giving in wasn't an option, as it never is for Tommy. Although he did what he could with the #3 for a while, he didn't know too well how to train with a gripper he couldn't close and wasn't really getting anywhere. He still found the #3 ridiculously hard, and there were times he thought he was simply too small to do this. In trying to find a solution, he decided to take one step back and purchase a #2 gripper as well (this one, by the way, he closed right away the first time he tried).

And there he was on his way to the #3 with a basic, but effective training regimen: He used the #2 for reps and did negatives with the #3, by using both hands to force it shut, letting go with the second hand and then trying to hang on with one hand, as the gripper slowly forced the hand open again.

More techniques and tools came into play over time (and we will cover them here). He experimented, stumbled, picked himself up, adjusted his training, and stubbornly pursued his goal for three years. Then, in the early summer of 2001, he finally certified for the #3 in front of two big, rough, and mighty strong judges: John Brookfield (hand strength pioneer, one of the first Captains of Crush® closers and Red Nail benders, and author of such classics as *Mastery of Hand Strength* and *The Grip Master's Manual*) and Steve Jeck (expert at the ancient art of Stone Lifting and author of the charming *Of Stones and Strength*). "It was cool to meet them. I did it so fast that I had to close it a couple times, because they weren't sure," Tommy remembers. Finally he got the certification, and I don't think John and Steve would have given their name as judges if it hadn't been legitimate.

Three years later he certified for the #4. "That was a monster," he says, and the monster left its traces: Tommy was so close to conquering the #4 for such a long time but not going anywhere that he decided to cut off all other training other than the gripper workouts. For 5-6 months he neglected all the other areas of grip strength and wrist strength he had been working on, until he finally managed to close the #4 and get his certification for it. But not without feeling a slight pain in his middle finger tendon coming on, which had started to plague him occasionally in the last few months. The pain got worse and eventually, right after certifying for the #4, he had to stop all of his training for about a year. And that middle finger tendon still pipes up from time to time, Tommy told me, especially when he gives the grippers another try these days. (If you want to avoid injuries of this kind before you get anywhere with the grippers, keep reading. We have included chapters in this book in which you can learn from Tommy's mistakes, so you don't have to go down that same road.)

Of course this setback doesn't stop Tommy from thinking up and performing other amazing feats of grip-, wrist-, or any other kind of oldtime strength (besides the fact that he doesn't have to prove anything any more when it comes to grippers, in my opinion). And we will cover some of those other feats of grip strength here as well, so you don't get too occupied with those nasty little grippers.

Tommy now lives with his wife, Mary Jo, in Front Royal, Virginia, and when he doesn't think up new twists on oldtime strongman or grip strength feats, he spends time with his twin boys. He is one of the friendliest and funniest guys I've ever talked to (I believe he performs all of his feats with a smile on his face), and definitely one of the most noteworthy "new oldtime strongmen" alive.

So read on and learn from the master.

Robert Spindler with Tommy Heslep

Grip Strength

3. GETTING STARTED

3.1. The Different Types of Grip Strength

In this chapter, we will explain the different types of grip strength that exist and how they can be categorized.

As you no doubt know, there are different kinds of hand- and grip strength and different ways of categorizing them. I will apply a simplified categorization of the most up-to-date categorization IronMind® uses. To make it simple, there are two types of grip strength:

A) Crushing grip
B) Pinch grip

A crushing grip means to use your palm and fingers to hold or "crush" an object in your hand, for example, closing a heavy gripper or holding a thick-handled barbell.

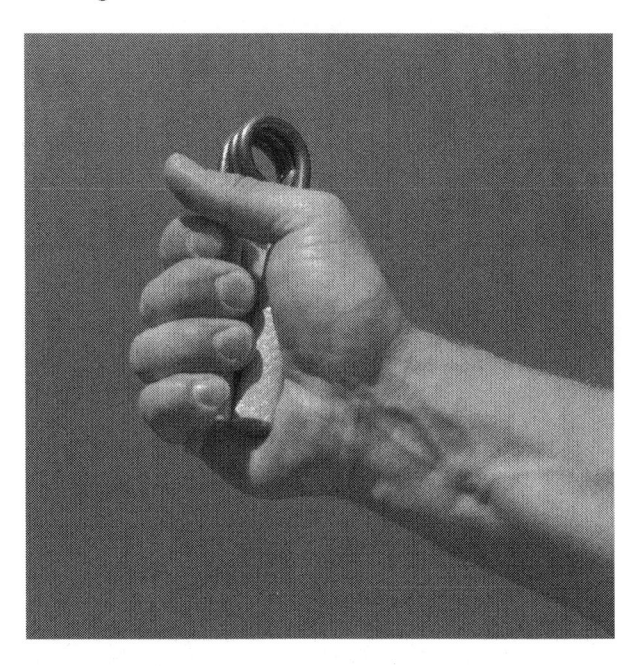

Fig. 3.1 Crushing grip: closing a gripper

A pinch grip means "pinching" an object between your fingers and your thumb, like picking up a board in one hand.

17

These are the two major movements, which you can then again train for two aims:

A) **Maximum strength**
B) **Endurance strength**

Maximum strength, you guessed it, is the maximum weight or resistance you can handle in one of these movements for one repetition, while **endurance strength** means to statically hold a weight or fight the resistance for as long as you can until failure, or doing a maximum number of repetitions.

Here we will focus primarily on maximum strength, because it is much more fun to train (we think) and progress is easier to determine, but also because training for maximum strength will automatically increase you endurance on all lifts as well (to a certain extent). Remember that Tommy's focus in training was almost always maximum strength, but that the feat of holding back two aeroplanes is basically a feat of endurance strength. Still, we will try to give endurance strength its deserved attention, as it is required in so many sports - just think of climbing or strongman sports.

IronMind® then makes another differentiation between **closed hand** and **open hand**. To imagine this, take the difference between lifting one 1 inch thick board between the thumb and fingers of one hand, or lifting four 1 inch thick boards in the same manner. In the first feat your hand is closed, in the latter it's open. For simplicity we will ignore this differentiation a little bit here, while still taking care that you train your grip in every major way. This basically involves different thicknesses of objects for training your pinch grip, a full range of motion when training your crushing grip, and some thick bar-lifting.

If you want to learn more about IronMind®'s grip strength categorization, do some research on the **Crushed-to-Dust!® Cube**. You might also want to look into the writings of John Brookfield, who is famous for his thorough and multifaceted approach towards grip strength training and his innovative exercises which train your hands from every imaginable angle.

For now just remember: there is the **crushing grip** and the **pinch grip**, which we will, in any case, train **both** (and I will tell you why in due course). We will train primarily for **maximum strength**, assuming that your endurance will increase along the way, but also focus on **endurance** occasionally. To not have to worry about closed and open hand positions, we will incorporate **thick bar-lifting** into our training (crushing grip, open hand), train with grippers in the **full range of motion**, always aiming to close them, but at least from a "credit card set" (this will be explained) (crushing grip, open to closed hand), and train our **pinch grip with various objects** ranging from large (open hand) to small (closed hand). If you train hard according to this variety, you should be able to excel in any kind of exotic grip strength challenge.

What we will not do is limit ourselves to only one very specific type of hand strength, like only trying to make progress on closing the grippers. Because, ignoring the thumb strength that is involved in thick bar-lifting and pinch grip exercises, for example, will not only make you prone to injuries, but actually curb your progress on the grippers as well. I will get back to this.

A note on the side: You may find different categorizations which list any number of grip strength types not listed here, but it always somehow comes down to those types IronMind® covers with the Crushed-to-Dust!® Cube. Let's take the strength of your finger tips as an example (typically utilized in rock climbing or when you attempt a chin-up on a small edge, on your finger tips only), which is often listed as a separate kind of grip strength. But imagine closing a Captains of Crush® Gripper without "setting" it, meaning you put it into your hand and try to close it from its fully extended position without any help from the other hand (what you would call a "no-set close" or "table no-set [TNS] close"). If your hands aren't toilet lid-sized, you would no doubt agree that this feat involves strength from your finger tips at the beginning of the movement. Or, imagine to pinch-grip an old-fashioned 45 lbs York barbell plate by its hub – isn't strength from your finger tips involved? So don't worry that we are missing out on any kind of major grip strength with this program.

Well ok, here is one more: the kind of strength you need to **extend your fingers**, that is, the very opposite movement of most grip exercises. This is not a kind of strength you will need for any particular feat of strength, and not even in everyday life, you might think. Still, we are not going to ignore it, as we want a balanced muscular development in our hands, mainly for health reasons. There are also other small muscles in your hand which we will "train" occasionally with low intensity, primarily for recovery and balance. More on this later.

As mentioned, this book is about grip strength, not wrist strength, although there is sometimes a smooth transition. Also, a strong grip and strong wrists and forearms go "hand in hand" (what a fitting idiom), so we will encourage you to train your wrists as well with some basic exercises at least.

Summary

- There are different types of grip strength which can be categorized in different ways. We distinguish between crushing grip and pinch grip...
- ...which can be trained for endurance or maximum strength...
- ...with open or closed hand.
- To cover all of these in our training, we will work with grippers, thick bar equipment, and differently sized objects in our pinch grip training.
- The strength required to open your hand, from your extensors, will also be trained.
- Likewise, wrist strength is a prerequisite for a strong grip and shouldn't be ignored as well.

3.2. Location

In this chapter we will give you some input and advice on how to choose your training location wisely.

Ok, so what kind of location do you need to train your grip effectively? A commercial gym? A garage? A repair shop? Or can you do it in your living room?

Well, the truth is you can train your grip just about anywhere. Tommy in fact did use his living room to build his insane grip strength. At first he went at it while watching TV!

When I asked him about the crucial detail whether he was sitting down or standing up while doing so, he told me that he would remain sitting on the couch until he got to work on the gripper he was trying to close at the time. Then he would stand up – and I think he would also not pay too much attention to the TV programme any more by then. I guess it shows you: While you can train your grip just about anywhere, you should have at least enough space to stand freely and you should be able to concentrate on it fully. That's why we don't recommend your car as your prime training location.

Here are some more thoughts on choosing your training location:

As your training progresses and gets more varied, it might involve the use of some **heavier equipment**, like barbell plates. So if you're blessed with a fine living room carpet or expensive floorboards you might want to consider moving to your basement or garage. You don't want the fear of dropping a barbell plate on your Persian carpet to stop you from squeezing out that new personal record on a pinch lift. In general, a location which can take some damage and dirt will be the better choice – also thinking about chalk for your record attempts.

A **sturdy table or work bench** in your training location is surely no mistake. Once you are using heavier plate-loaded grip strength machines you will need a place to put them or fix them to.

If you are training in a **commercial gym**, this has pros and cons. The good thing is, dumbbells, barbell plates, benches, etc. will be there in great variety and abundance. In all likelihood, chalk will be available, and dropping a barbell plate on the floor won't be much of a problem (if this isn't the case, you have probably chosen the wrong gym in the first place). The downsides are: you will neither want to carry your grip strength machines with you to the gym all the time if you are using any. Nor will you want to explain to every guy who walks past why you are maltreating that harmless little hand gripper with so much effort. Regular people in a commercial gym might not see the seriousness in your grip strength training and chat you up on last Sunday's game while you're seriously attempting to squeeze those gripper handles closer together than last week by one sixteenth of an inch. My advice: be polite, but firm. If they talk to you while you're training, you have every right to ignore them and then answer their questions when your set is done. In time, they will learn.

I think it doesn't hurt to settle on **one location** and stick to it as your "grip strength gym". Surely, if you're training at home you might want to step outside on a sunny day and perform your workout on the pavement, as Tommy did occasionally. But you will realize if you carry your grippers around with you all the time, believing you can get an efficient workout waiting for the bus or during your lunch break, you will not be able to focus in the same manner, because your training location constantly changes. Adapting to a new environment always takes energy away from your training and doesn't let you work out as efficiently (not to mention that you might need more than a just few grippers for an all-round grip workout).

At the end of the day, however, it simply depends on your own preference where you perform your workouts. You might want to train alone, with your buddies, in a fancy gym, or in your garage. As long as the atmosphere leads you towards peak performance, that's fine. If you need inspiration, check out the home gym of another supreme grip strength athlete of our time, Joe Kinney (the first man who got certified for closing the #4 Captains of Crush® Gripper). His home-made *Get a Grip* video, now available on DVD at www.functionalhandstrength.com, was shot there. I can assure you, it is nothing like a commercial fitness club.

But before you decide on your training location, read on. In the next chapter we will give you an idea of what basic equipment a "grip strength gym" should have.

Summary
- You can train your grip just about anywhere where you have enough space to stand freely and can concentrate on your workout without diversions.
- Preferably, though, choose a location where the floor can take some damage and dirt.
- A sturdy work bench or table in your training location is a plus, and becomes a must when you start using machines.
- A commercial gym has the advantage of available equipment such as barbell plates, dumbbells, and chalk, but the downside of limited freedom and sometimes difficulties to concentrate.
- Switch training locations as little as possible and try to stick to your one "grip strength gym".

3.3. Tools

In this chapter we will give you an idea of what pieces of equipment you will need to train your grip effectively and completely.

Your plans to finally purchase your own private heavy duty hand gripper might have inspired you to buy this book, or you might already have the one or the other lying around at home and now want to know how to close the stupid little things.

However, those grippers, and especially that *one* gripper, might not be sufficient to train your grip effectively - although they may be the best single tool to strengthen your grip (if you have the right one according to your level of strength).

Here is a list of things you should have at hand to perform all-encompassing, high intensity grip strength workouts.

1) Hand grippers

Still the best way to train your crushing grip. The IronMind® Captains of Crush® are the market leaders, and the epitome of heavy duty hand grippers. We will speak of them as *the* grippers here, although any quality heavy duty grippers from a comparable company, such as Beef Builder (BB), Heavy Grips (HG), GHP, used ones from the company PDA (which stopped producing in 2004), or the ones produced by Robert Baraban (RB) will do. Grippers from one or the other company might suit your purse better, others might offer more convenient steps of resistance.

What's more important than the company from which you buy is that once you have decided to get serious on your grip strength training, you need the right amount of grippers at the right levels of resistance according to your strength. Here, the common view is that you need **at least three grippers**: one as a sort of warm-up gripper with which you can do 10 reps or more; one for your working sets, meaning you can do 2-9 reps with it; and one is going to be your challenge gripper, meaning you want to close it next but can't yet.

For a beginner, this could be a CoC® #1 to warm up, a #1.5 for working sets, and a #2 as the challenge gripper. Or, for an advanced athlete, a #1 to warm up, a #2 for working sets, and a #3 as the challenge gripper. To determine which grippers you will need, IronMind® has a buying guide which makes sense, and so does www.functionalhandstrength.com. If you are still unsure, my advice is to buy just one of them (for example a #2) and play around with it a little - soon you'll know whether this is going to be your warm-up, working, or challenge gripper.

Remember Tommy, who first bought the #3. Once he realized he couldn't close it yet and hence couldn't really work on it effectively, he went and purchased a #2, a #1 and a "Trainer" as well.

Talking about the "Trainer", which IronMind® introduced as one step below the #1: You might also want to buy **a fourth gripper** for a low intensity warm-up prior to the warm-up with the gripper we talked about above. One with which you can do 20 reps or more. This doesn't necessarily have to be a high quality, heavy duty gripper from one of the companies mentioned. For a low intensity warm-up, your cheap plastic hand gripper from the local sporting goods store will suffice. We'll get back to warm-up later.

Once you have closed your challenge gripper, of course, you might want to go and buy the next one.

2) Strap

Easy to come by, yet making for a very effective workout, is a simple, but strong **strap of fabric or leather, for strap holds**. This is a static exercise, invented by John Brookfield (as so many). You fix a small amount of weight to a flat strap, which you then squeeze between the handles of a gripper you can close with not too much effort. Then you try to lift the weight while holding the gripper shut. You then hold it as long as possible, keeping the strap from slipping out from between the handles and thus the weight from dropping to the ground, by squeezing the handles together as hard as you can.

IronMind® sells standardized straps in two thicknesses used for grip strength contests. I think a simple leather strap, about 1 inch (2.5 cm) wide and preferably as thin as possible, yet strong enough to hold some weight, will do for "home use". We will get back to strap holds in the training section.

3) Barbell plates

Preferably with at least one smooth side and 2 inch (50 mm) holes (I will tell you why). You will need barbell plates for all kinds of grip exercises, most prominently for pinch grip training - that's why it is preferred for them to have at least one smooth side. This way you can put two together and have a perfect object to train and test your pinch grip - just pinch the two plates with thumb and fingers and try to lift them.

But you will need all varieties of barbell plates for loads of different exercises, such as "strap holds" or for thick bar lifting. That's why it's best to have **a range of barbell plate pairs**, from the very lightest to the 45 lbs (20 kg) ones.

The 2 inch (50 mm) holes are not a must, but preferred simply because they are more compatible with most modern equipment, and also because they can be combined with a simple piece of equipment to do thick bar lifts. To find out what I mean, read on.

However, if you don't have easy access to barbell plates or don't want to make an investment yet, you will get pretty far by using buckets filled with stones, water or sand as additional weight, as Tommy did when he started out. But after some time you might either find they are not convenient enough or do not offer enough resistance. Find out for yourself to what extent you can improvise.

4) Wooden blocks

This is the way Tommy started out with his **pinch grip training**: he took two wooden blocks, a 2 inch x 4 inch (5 cm x 10 cm) and a 4 inch x 4 inch (10 cm x 10 cm), drilled a hole through each, hooked a cable to them and added any weight, like a bucket of sand. Two fairly simple tools which you can carry around in your gym bag, with a lot of advantages for pinch grip training. The two different sizes allow you to work your pinch grip with open and closed hand, and the adjustable weight allows you to work ahead in small steps, where pinching barbell plates would limit you in several ways. Especially if you don't have barbell plates yet, this is the way to go to train your pinch grip effectively.

5) Thick bar equipment

A thick bar handle can vary anywhere from a 2 inch (5 cm) to 3 inch (8 cm) diameter, and, obviously, the thicker the handle the heavier a weight will be to lift. If you want some kind of standard, the Rolling Thunder® Revolving Deadlift Handle is 2 3/8 inches (6 cm) in diameter, and the Inch Dumbbell is about the same.

To train your grip strength via thick bar lifts, the **Rolling Thunder® Revolving Deadlift Handle**, available on the IronMind® homepage and at various dealers, is a great tool which allows you to vary the weight you are lifting simply by adding plates. There are also official competitions which test your open hand crushing grip with this exact device, so if you plan to enter grip strength contests, you might find this a reasonable investment.

A cheaper alternative are the popular **Fat Gripz**™, two rubber handles you can slip on almost any standard barbell or dumbbell, effectively widening their handles to 2 to 2.5 inches (5 cm to 6.5 cm). They allow you to do basically any exercise with a "thick bar", from deadlifts to barbell curls. Obviously, you will not be able to lift the same overall weight as without the Fat Gripz™ because you are limited by your grip strength. But you will surely build a monster grip if you use them regularly. Especially if you work out in a gym which has a good dumbbell rack with dumbbells at least up to 110 lbs (50 kg) and beyond, you can slip the Fat Gripz™ on dumbbells and work towards deadlifting the Baby Inch or the Inch dumbbell, both recognized benchmark feats of grip strength. If you train in a commercial gym where you can find a rope pulley handle which is wide enough, you can slip a Fatgrip onto it and thus create your own cheap Rolling Thunder® replacement (not quite the same, perhaps, but a way to train and test your thick bar strength before buying a genuine Rolling Thunder®).

A still cheaper and very simple way to do thick bar workouts, especially if you are fond of home-made training equipment and have access to scrap metal, is to get hold of **two sturdy iron pipes**, the first one with a 2 inch (5 cm) diameter and about 20 inches (50 cm) in length, the second one with an inside diameter slightly above 2 inches and an outside diameter of anything up to 3 inches (8 cm) (basically the thick bar diameter you want to work with) at a length of about 5 inches (13 cm), or the length of a dumbbell handle you feel comfortable working with. The way to work with these is to slip the thicker pipe onto the thinner one, so that it is in the middle of the thinner one, and then load the thinner one with barbell plates until you have the desired weight (this is one of the reasons why I advised you to purchase 2 inch (50 mm) hole barbell plates if you can). Secure the plates on the pipe with collars as you would on a regular barbell, and there you have your thick bar dumbbell with variable weight. The upside of this tool (apart from that it is very cheap if you have the right source for scrap metal), is that you can load a large amount of weight onto it, where the Fat Gripz™ limit you to the weight of the heaviest dumbbell you can find. You can also use this tool for another effective exercise as well: by tying a simple short rope with a weight plate at its end onto the longer, inside pipe, you can do wrist rolls, strengthening your wrists by rolling the weight up while holding the pipe in front of you with both hands.

One of the most classic thick bar grip strength feats is deadlifting the **Inch dumbbell**, or, God beware, lifting it overhead with one hand (awfully few men have achieved this "officially"). For "beginners", there is always the lighter Baby Inch to approach one of these feats. If you are interested in the myths surrounding Thomas Inch's challenge dumbbell, you might want to get hold of a replica of the Inch or the Baby Inch (hard to get), or a Circus Dumbbell, as the ones used in Strongman competitions are called. The latter are easier to get hold of and are either available in various fixed weights, or can be filled or plate loaded to any amount of weight you wish (depending on the material you fill them with). If you are a handyman, you can also build your own (Baby) Inch replica using concrete, as Tommy did. It will turn our larger in size than the original Inch dumbbells, but it will look darn good in

6) Rubber bands

These are needed to train the muscles in your hands and forearms which **open your hand** as opposed to closing them, as all other grip exercises do. You need to train these muscles, the extensors, mainly for balance and injury prevention - but don't think it is something which can be ignored! Complicated devices to train these extensors exist, but the simplest and most common way is to use rubber bands. As rubber bands you can practically use anything you can find which offers enough resistance. I used rubber rings for those old fashioned Mason jars with glass lids for a while, but you can also tie several regular rubber bands together, or you can use rubber bracelets, or rubber hairbands. I have to admit, though, that the material the original IronMind® Expand-Your-Hand Bands™ are made of feels absolutely best (although they can and do snap if you use them a lot). They also have a very constant resistance as you extend them, other than most rubber bands you will find. However, if you want to save money you will find a way to improvise. A cheap but less mobile alternative would be a bucket of rice or sand (see chapter 8).

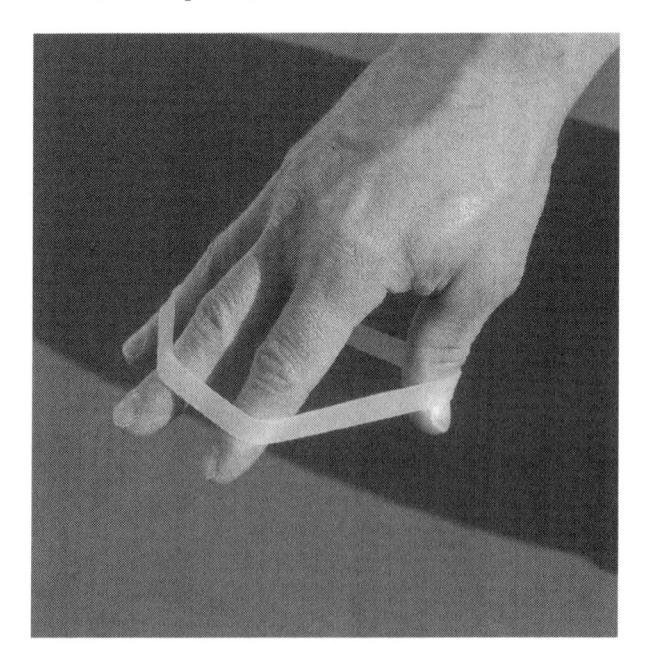

Fig. 3.2 A mason jar rubber ring functioning as a training tool for the hand extensors

7) Dumbbells, barbells

While not necessary by all means to train your grip, dumbbells and barbells are the standard tools to train all other muscles in your body. While some say that training larger muscle groups like legs has helped them to improve their grip strength, this isn't a must (Tommy didn't). But you should at least work on your wrist strength parallel to your grip strength training. First of all for muscle balance and hand health, and secondly to assist you in feats like thick bar lifting. There are other ways to train your wrists and forearms, but the most basic exercises are performed with dumbbells and barbells.

Also, you can warm-up your whole body for a grip strength session with a pair of dumbbells. This might become a necessity, as you will hear later.

8) Chalk

Not a necessity (Tommy didn't use it, and many other grip strength athletes did neither), but helpful if you tend to have sweaty hands or live in a hot climate. It keeps the grippers from slipping out of your hands. Also, if you don't use it in your regular training, you might want to use it for personal record attempts. For some it becomes a mere psychological device: in the end, they won't be able to close the Trainer without chalk on their hands.

> **Hint:**
> **If you regularly use chalk when training with grippers, clean them with a wire brush from time to time. If you don't, all the chalk stuck on the gripper handles will make them more slippery.**

3.3.1. Advanced Tools

Now I have given you a list of seven items which I believe are basic tools indispensable for an all-encompassing grip strength workout. But here are two more tools you might want to get hold of as your training progresses:

9) Grip machine

It may sound like a paradox, but although quality hand grippers are among the best tools to strengthen your grip in themselves, a plate-loaded grip machine is indispensable if you really want to make progress on closing a gripper as tough as a #3 or above. This needs to be a machine which imitates the movement of closing a standard gripper closely, so take care to choose one which has handles about the size of your grippers and arranged at about the same angle when open and closed. The advantages of such a grip machine are: A) The possibility of adjusting the resistance by small steps by loading or unloading barbell plates, B) the possibility of using great amounts of weight for effective negatives (with a different dynamic than simply a heavier gripper), C) probably most importantly: the possibility to train **beyond the range**, that is, filed off ends on the handles, in order to squeeze them even closer together than the handles of a regular gripper.

Let me explain this last point: If you have trained with heavy duty grippers before, you will know that **the very last part of the movement**, the last few millimetres before the gripper "closes", **is the hardest**, also because the gripper increases resistance as the handles move closer together. It is difficult to work on that last part on the movement effectively, for example with negatives with a harder gripper you force shut with two hands and then try to hold shut with one hand, because the gripper will immediately force your hand open by a few millimetres before you have a chance to fight the resistance at all. You will never get a chance to effectively train this most important part of the movement.

If, however, you have a grip machine which allows you to work even beyond this last part of the movement, you will eventually get stronger within the decisive range when you try to close a gripper. The diameter of a Captains of Crush® Gripper handle is roughly 3/4 inches (19.5 mm), so when you close a heavy gripper you are squeezing an "object" of about 1.5 inches (39 mm), and it will appear rather tough to do that. But if your grip machine allows you to squeeze the filed off handles together to, say, an "object" of 1 inch (25 mm), and you frequently train within that range, **the last part of the movement** of closing the same gripper as above **will appear relatively easy**.

Powerlifters do the same when they do deadlifts standing on an elevated platform (with the barbell still on the floor). They train beyond the range in order to increase their strength at the foremost part of the movement, that is, lifting the barbell off the ground.

If you are looking for a simple way to have this one advantage, you can also **grind off the ends of the handles** of a gripper you can close for a few reps already. Also, if you train in a commercial gym, you will not be able to carry a massive grip machine with you all the time - then this will be the way to go.

Fig. 3.3 A gripper with part of the handle filed off - note the tape on the one handle which helps preserving the skin on you hand when doing negatives

However, if you don't like the idea of messing up the expensive grippers and are keen on the other advantages of a grip machine as well, here are some suggestions:

The machine Tommy used was the infamous "**Gripanator**" from the company PDA. It's a massive hulk of a machine which you can load with Olympic barbell plates. However, they are not being produced any more. But there are imitations. One of them can be found as "**Extreme Grip Machine**" in the UK (It is also "extremely" expensive, by the way). Both the original Gripanator and the Extreme Grip Machine have ground off handles.

Fig. 3.4 The Gripanator

A simpler alternative (but not much less expensive) is the **Go-Really-Grip™ Machine by IronMind®**, the classic floor-model grip machine, which has a wider range of motion than a Captains of Crush® Gripper as well and can be loaded with lots of Olympic barbell plates (notice that all of these machines work with Olympic barbell plates? That's another reason why I recommended purchasing those). However, you will need more plates than with a Gripanator-like machine because the IronMind® floor-model grip machine has no leverage effect. I have also heard complaints that it puts your hands at awkward angles, not resembling the motion of hand grippers closely enough. It is surely a quality product, though, built to last.

Another alternative is to **build your own grip machine**. If you are good with your hands, have some welding skill, and access to scrap metal, you might get away with a comfortable, cheap, and highly effective grip machine, custom-made according to your needs. Watch Joe Kinney's *Get A Grip* for inspiration. He has an amazing array of home-made grip machines, and you will marvel at how simple some of them are, yet how effectively they work. In my opinion, his "Secret Weapon" is the one machine which combines all advantages mentioned above, yet it is fairly easy to be made at home. Which is what I did. My model is smaller and very transportable. I can carry it with me in my gym bag wherever I go, and simply fix it to a sturdy power rack with a small c-clamp. Be creative.

10) Thumb machine/Jewel

Pinch grip exercises and thick bar training are the easiest ways to strengthen your thumb, but they are all static holds which do not challenge your thumb muscles across a full range of motion. To compensate, many elite grip strength athletes incorporate dynamic thumb exercises into their training. The most straightforward way to do so is to purchase a specialized plate-loaded machine, available from IronMind®, called "**Titan's Telegraph Key**™," which uses a great angle to target your thumbs.

Still, it is a very specialized tool and you might figure it too much of an investment to work something as "unimportant" as your thumbs only. The latter part of that argument is nonsense, of course, as your thumb is very important for any grip strength feat. Yes, even for the grippers, as strongly developed thumb muscles prevent the gripper from slipping from your palm. I have some understanding for the first, the financial part of the argument, though.

For that part, you may either want to build your own Telegraph Key-like machine, or your own "**Jewel**", a simple but brilliant tool invented by Tommy and partly inspired by his father. It consists of two small and thin wooden boards, parallel to each other, and connected by four springs and bolts. You can use it effectively to **target your thumbs**, do **dynamic pinch grip training**, and to train the hand position used for **card tearing** (the original reason why Tommy invented the tool).

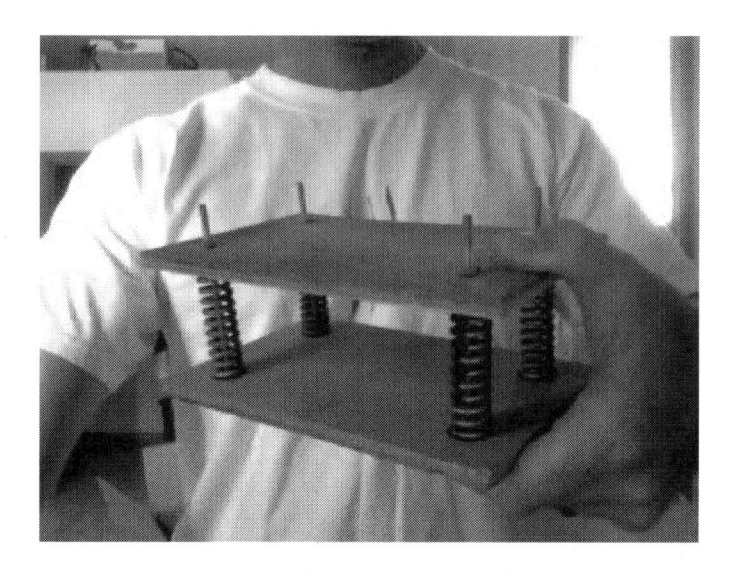

Fig. 3.5 Tommy with the original "Jewel"

If you purchase several sets of springs with varying dynamics, you can easily adjust the resistance as well (although you would have to fumble around a bit with the small screws and bolts). Again, the jewel is something small enough to carry around in your gym bag (realize how that bag starts to fill?) and something you can build on your own for a few bucks worth of material, or for free if you have access to scrap metal and wood.

3.3.2. Tools for Recovery
Here are some items you might want to have at hand for a quick recovery session on your rest days.

11) Rubber ball
What used to be considered a grip strength workout on its own – that therapy rubber ball you purchased at your local sporting goods store a few years ago – will now have to give way to your heavy duty grippers for a serious workout. But don't throw it away. It's still **useful for recovery**, that is, for a light workout that helps you to recuperate and go into your next heavy workout fully recovered.

If you don't have one of those already, they are available at most sporting goods stores and will be the second thing the clerk will offer if you if you ask for grip strength training equipment (the first will be a plastic-handled spring gripper). They are relatively cheap compared to most professional grip strengthening tools and convenient to keep in your car for a light recovery workout on the way to work.

A similar grip strength tool used to be en vogue some time ago, made not of elastic rubber but of a foamy substance. You can knead it in your hand like clay (Sylvester Stallone can be seen playing around with one of those in the movie *Over the Top*). Maybe your uncle still has one of those lying around somewhere and if you are lucky he can be persuaded to pass it on to you.

You can also purchase an **IronMind® EGG**, which were specially designed for that purpose and are available in various levels of resistance.

12) Two 5 gallon buckets

Or any two bowls, pots, or whatever can be filled with water and is large enough to submerge your hands and wrists in. These will be used for contrast baths.

Shouldn't be too much of a problem to get hold of those.

13) Sledge hammer

A wonderful tool (not just for workouts). Most commonly used for wrist strength, it can be used for "finger walking" (another one of John Brookfield's inventions, I believe), an exercise that reaches all of the little muscles in your hand we haven't covered yet (remember that muscle balance is important). But as we already agreed that wrist strength can't hurt to boost healthy grip strength, and as loads of other pretty exercises can be performed with it, consider your sledge hammer a multifunctional tool around the gym – and house.

Before you go to your local hardware store to pick one up, memorize the exercises we will cover below and try which size and weight suits you best to perform them (be prepared to get some funny looks). In case of doubt, go for the heavier or larger one, as we expect your grip and wrist strength to increase considerably within the next few months.

Also, if you don't have a sledge hammer at home already, don't go out and purchase one right away (can be expensive), just because you read it here. It's not the most important tool and, by the way, you can do most sledge-hammer-exercises with an empty (non-Olympic) 20 lbs (10 kg) barbell as well, if you happen to have one.

But if you have other uses for it as well, if you are a handyman and like to fix and build things around the house yourself, you might figure the investment well worth it.

Fig. 3.6 Some items you could have in your personal grip strength gym (from left to right, top to bottom): weight bar, sledge hammer, weights, plastic bowls for contrast baths, leather strap for strap holds, plastic-handled gripper for warm-ups, heavy duty warm-up gripper, heavy duty working gripper, heavy duty challenge gripper, heavy duty gripper for negatives, rubber ball, rubber bands for hand extensor training, thumb machine, grip machine for beyond-the-range training

> **Hint:**
> There are lots of fancy, popular grip strength tools on the market which I didn't mention (I see mostly hobby rock climbers using those). While all of them can be put to use - for warm-up, regeneration or endurance work at the least - don't be fooled by clever marketing into thinking they are in any way superior to the tools I have listed. The tools I have listed are the basics, they can either be home-made or purchased from different companies, and they will allow you to work your grip from every angle you need with the intensity you need, for a lifetime. No single tool can do this, especially if it's made of plastic.

Summary
- Eight basic tools have been recommended for an all-round grip strength training:
    1. **Heavy duty spring-handled grippers** (at least three of them: one for warm-ups, one for working sets, one as a challenge)
    2. **Straps** for strap holds
    3. **Barbell plates** as resistance for all kinds of exercises
    4. **Wooden blocks** for pinch grip training
    5. **Thick Bar Equipment** for open hand crushing grip training
    6. **Rubber bands** to work the hand extensors (or a bucket of rice or sand)
    7. **Dumbbells, Barbells,** for various additional exercises, especially wrist exercises, and for warm-up
    8. **Chalk** for sweaty hands and record attempts
- Two tools have been recommended for advanced grip strength athletes:
    9. **Grip machine,** for heavy negatives, adjusted steps in increasing resistance, and beyond-the-range training
    10. **Thumb machine** or home-made **Jewel,** for effective dynamic thumb training and pinch grip preparation
- Three tools have been suggested for recovery sessions:
    11. **Rubber ball** for light recovery workouts
    12. **Two 5 gallon buckets** for contrast baths
    13. **Sledge hammer,** for finger walking, but also for additional wrist strength workouts

3.4. Warm-Up

Read in this chapter how to warm-up correctly and safely for a hardcore grip strength training session.

There are guys who don't warm up at all and others who warm up forever before a grip strength training session. Tommy belongs to the latter.

And we recommend that you join this group as well. Remember, we are only telling you what worked for Tommy and it must not necessarily work for everyone. But **a proper warm-up**, to err on the side of cautiousness, **is never a bad idea**. Better be safe than sorry.

Tommy's warm-up would usually take **15-20 minutes**, sometimes even more. Considering that his grip strength sessions would generally take him about an hour altogether, including warm-up, you realize how important the warm-up was for him – consuming at least a quarter of his workout time.

The way he went about it was pretty straight forward: he did **sets of ten with each of the lighter grippers**, going from the lightest to the hardest, alternating hands.

Let's say he was at a stage where he couldn't close the #4 yet, and could close the #3 for three or four reps. He would start with the Trainer, closing it ten times with his weaker, his left hand, then with his right hand (it is always a good idea to start with your weaker hand, else the imbalance between your hands will increase over time). After a short break he would continue with the #1: ten reps left hand, ten reps right hand. Then the same with the #2. The real workout would then begin with the work on the #3. (If you can close the #3 for three or four times, ten reps with the #2 is clearly only a warm-up, in case you wonder.)

This is a pretty standard warm-up routine which should be the least you do. Obviously, you don't necessarily need three warm-up grippers. If the #2.5 is your challenge gripper, ten reps with the Trainer followed by ten reps with the #1 will do (followed by working sets with the #2, for example). Alternately, if you don't have a Trainer and think two warm-up grippers aren't worth the investment, you can use a light, plastic-handled gripper from your local sporting goods store instead (as I have explained above). But remember that a lighter Captains of Crush® Gripper prepares you better for a heavier Captains of Crush® than any other gripper (the same is true for heavy duty grippers of any other brand). Also remember that even Tommy used the Trainer for a warm-up although he was on his way to develop one of the strongest grips in the world. So don't think you're too tough for the Trainer.

A few more pieces of advice for the warm-up:

One day, after a warm-up of this kind, Tommy picked up the #3 to begin his training proper. He got up from his sofa (where he would perform his warm-up), got into a good stance and squeezed that #3 mercilessly. Suddenly he felt a pain creeping from his finger tips all the way through to his back and neck. He explains: "I felt that pain in my back and neck and realized: I'm not just using my hand muscles here, I'm using everything, my whole upper body." From that day on, he performed **an additional upper-body warm-up** before he went into the heavy sets. He did a few exercises with one of those therapy rubber bands, did some push-ups, and a few dumbbell curls, to get the blood circulation in all the muscles in his upper body going before he would tackle the heavy grippers. And his workouts got better.

So, we advise you to do at least some push-ups and rubber band or dumbbell exercises as part of your warm up, for example in between your gripper warm-up sets (that way you won't lose time).

If you are a strength athlete or bodybuilder, or perform a general weight training anyway, it is recommended to perform your grip strength training right after your regular workout sessions. That way your upper body will be properly warmed up already. But don't forget to perform your grip strength-specific warm-up as well – always use those lighter grippers to prepare for the heavier ones.

There are strength athletes and bodybuilders who warm up their hamstrings with a light set of 20 leg curls before they go into a heavy quadriceps or squat workout. Following the same logic, it is surely no bad idea to **warm up your hand extensors** with a light set of rubber band extensions, using the rubber bands we introduced in the "Tools" section above. One light set of 10-20 reps will do. You will feel a comfortable contrast to all the "hand-closing" of your other warm-up sets, and only then you will have the feeling that all the muscles in your hand are properly warmed up. Try it.

Just remember the importance of a proper warm-up. **Don't ever touch your challenge gripper if you are not prepared** - not to try something you just saw in a Youtube video, and not to impress your friends who challenge you to demonstrate what you have been rigorously training for the last few weeks. Just don't do it unless you are warmed up. In the best case, you will not be as strong as you would have been with a proper warm-up. In the worst case, you will hurt yourself and lose weeks of training time.

Again, there are people who don't warm up at all, but for Tommy it worked best to always do. Just grabbing the #3 and trying really wouldn't go too good. So we recommend that you warm up as well.

> **Hint:**
> **I'm not the only one who uses a mouth guard for an extra heavy grip strength session on occasion. Unconsciously biting your teeth during severe reps or negatives can cause dental damage over the years.**

Summary
- Always warm up before a grip strength session.
- When training with grippers, do sets of tens with (at least two) lighter grippers before you go into your working sets with the heavier grippers. Work both hands alternately, beginning with your weaker hand.
- Make sure your whole upper body is warmed up before a hardcore grip strength workout, either by a regular weight training or by light upper-body exercises.
- Warm up your hand extensors as well with a light set of rubber band extensions.

3.5. Frequency

In this chapter we will give you some ideas on how frequently you should train your grip.

For Tommy, quite clearly, it worked best to train his grip **twice a week**. Usually, he would work his grip (crushing and pinch grip combined in one session) on Mondays and Thursdays. Besides grip strength, Tommy is also an expert in steel bending and other feats of wrist strength. So he would use the same amount of time to **train his wrists**: Tuesdays and Fridays were wrist strength days. Wednesdays and the weekend were rest days. Workouts would take one hour, including warm-up.

In sum, this is a quite well-arranged and straightforward split training which you could follow:

Monday: **Grip** (crushing and pinch)
Tuesday: Wrists
Wednesday: Rest
Thursday: **Grip** (crushing and pinch)
Friday: Wrists
Saturday: Rest
Sunday: Rest

It gives you full strength to attack your grip on Monday after two days of rest and recovery on the weekend. There is enough time between the two grip days to recuperate, and you are not lazy on all of the other days of the week, using two for useful additional training. Remember, even if you are not interested in wrist strength feats, strong and healthy wrists and forearms are part of an elite grip.

Some additional thoughts on frequency: Tommy experimented a bit, trying to do more per week, but he soon realized it was to no benefit. Going at it with his kind of intensity, his hands would ache all the time once he trained more often than twice per week. So don't make this beginner's mistake of thinking 'more is better'.

The same applies to the **duration** of each single workout. **One hour**, including warm-up, is usually enough. Remember that Tommy's workouts took no longer than that although he warmed up for 15-20 minutes, and although he now admits he might have done too much at some points in time. He admits that he sometimes did way too many sets, where much less would have sufficed. The advice he gives now, after more than a decade of grip strength experience, is: "Get in, hit it hard and get out."

It's as simple as that. I know you are longing to get up right now and crush those little things. I know you would like to work your grip every day if you could. But retain that energy. Focus it on that one hour when it is needed: Then you can let it all go. Remember that your muscles get stronger during rest days, not during workouts.

But again: what has been described is what worked best for Tommy. It might not work best for you, although we believe that this kind of routine would work best for a majority of trainees. So don't be afraid to experiment:

For example: did you have to skip one of your Thursday grip strength workouts lately and were surprisingly stronger than ever the next Monday? Then maybe two sessions per week is too much for you and you would fare better with only one per week. Nothing to be ashamed of. Leaves you more time to work the rest of your body.

Or did you have to throw in another grip strength session on Saturday, because you simply couldn't do without your little grippers for a whole weekend? But you were as strong as ever again on Monday, without negative effects? Then three times per week might be ok for you.

Try to find out what's best for you. Realize: on the one hand, we are all individuals, but on the other hand we are all the same base model. Meaning that: you might have your own ideal frequency of grip strength sessions per week, but it will be within certain limits. More than three hardcore grip strength sessions per week will be too many for anyone except genetic freaks, and less than one session per week... forget it.

> **Hint:**
> **Your ability to recuperate from strength workouts can also vary with age. As Russian world-class powerlifters have pointed out to me, their teenage athletes train as frequently as six days per week, twice a day, whereas an athlete in his late twenties - even world champions - will do with a total of three sessions per week.**

Summary

- We recommend that you train your grip (crushing grip and pinch grip in one session) twice per week, on separate days, with two to three rest days in between.
- You may want to experiment a bit to find out what's ideal for you. Maybe once or three times per week is your perfect frequency. But we don't believe that much more or much less than that will bring the desired results.
- For the duration of each workout, including warm-up, one hour is a good guideline. You might need a bit less or a bit more than that, but focus on intensity rather than quantity.
- Again, these are guidelines and you need to find out what's best for you.

4. CRUSHING GRIP: CLOSING HEAVY-DUTY GRIPPERS

This chapter focuses on the crushing grip, the dynamic strength required to squeeze an object in your hand. It tells you how to train effectively with heavy-duty spring handled grippers.

Now let's really get started. This chapter is all about the crushing grip. We will train it primarily with spring handled grippers, because we figure it the best training tool to develop this kind of grip strength. But we will also cover supplementary machine work.

We will always focus on training in order to "close" heavy duty grippers from a "credit card set" (this will be explained), not only because it is a convenient and - for the IronMind® grippers - official way to test and measure your grip strength, but also because it forces you to train your grip along a full range of motion.

4.1. The Captains of Crush® Grippers: Some History, Mystery and Fact on Gripper Certification

This chapter aims to give a short overview of some important chapters in the history of the Captains of Crush® certification lists. It also addresses some rumours surrounding the grippers.

As the IronMind® Captains of Crush® grippers where the first heavy duty grippers of their kind available to the broad public, I think a short comment on some of the mysteries they spawned is appropriate. The reason why I will keep this account as short as possible is because a wonderful book has been published on the topic before, which covers the history of the grippers in great detail and also contains useful chapters on gripper training: *The Captains of Crush® Grippers: What they are and How to Close Them*, by Randall J. Strossen, J.B. Kinney, and Nathan Holle. Consult it if you want to know more.

What I want to focus on is basically the history of the list of people who closed the #3, #3.5, and #4 grippers, as this basic knowledge might make some of the other things in this book a bit clearer.

As you, in all likelihood, know by now, you get a certification by IronMind® and an honourable mention on their website if you succeed in closing (squeezing the two handles together in one hand so that they touch) either the #3, #3.5, or the #4 gripper in front of (an) appointed judge(s). These certification lists can be viewed on the IronMind® webpage at http://www.ironmind.com/ironmind/opencms/Main/captainsofcrush3.html

(this is the list for the #3 - on the page you will find the links to the #3.5 and #4). But what you need to know is, the rules of how such a close should be performed to be official changed over the years.

The first person to have closed the #3 was Richard Sorin in 1991, soon after the Captains of Crush® Grippers came out (he was followed by the legendary John Brookfield in 1992). Now if you look closely at the list, you notice that there is another Richard Sorin on it in 2007. Yes, he is the same person. The story behind this is that **the rules have changed considerably over the years**, and Richard Sorin, famed for having been the first to close the #3, stepped on the scene again to prove he could still do it - old rules, new rules, either way.

How did the rules change, and what was so significant about these changes that Richard felt he would have to prove he could still close the #3 by the new rules? In the early 2000s, Bill Piche established the **Gripboard**, an Internet community on grip strength, and produced tutorials on how to close the Captains of Crush® Grippers after short periods of training. One of his most essential pieces of advice was to set the gripper in the palm of your hand (with the help of the other hand) so that you could exert the greatest amount of force on it through the best possible leverage. Basically, this meant setting it in such a way that the handles were already considerably close together once you started your attempt with the one hand only. Sometimes this meant that the handles were as much as parallel to each other at the beginning of the movement - sometimes they were even closer. This proved highly effective and made it considerably easier to close the grippers. The number of those who certified for the #3 rose.[1]

Yes, it rose to such an extent that IronMind® felt closing the grippers with this technique was too easy. They experimented for some time with various rule changes. At first they established that the gripper handles must be at least 1 inch (c. 2.5 cm) apart at the beginning of the movement. Eventually, though, they settled on the following rule:

> 4. The free hand may be used to position the gripper in the gripping hand, but the starting position can be no narrower than the width of a credit/ATM card, and the gripster must show the official that he has an acceptable starting position by using his non-gripping hand to slide the end of a credit/ATM card in between the ends of the handles. Once this is done, the official will give the signal to remove

---

[1] Yes, also Tommy certified for the #3 during that time - but we have seen him close the #3 with a no-set close - without any help of the other hand at all - several times, so no need to question him. By the way, it is still not that easy a feat to close the #3 even with a parallel set.

the card and begin the attempt. Any contact between the non-gripping hand and the gripper as the card is being removed will invalidate the attempt, and the non-gripping hand must stay at least a foot from the gripping hand at all times during the squeeze. Similarly, nothing may be in contact with the gripping hand or the gripping arm from the elbow down (for example, the free hand is not allowed to steady the wrist of the gripping hand or hold the spring, etc.). The entire squeeze must be clearly visible to the official: the gripper cannot be closed while blocked from view and then turned and presented as already closed.[2]

A credit card is about 2.175 inches in width (c. 5.4 cm), meaning that the gripper handles must be that far apart before you attempt your close. The first part of this rule is popularly referred to as the "**credit card rule**". And a "**credit card set**" (short: CCS) means that you attempt to close a gripper according to this rule (a "deep set" means that the handles are much less apart in general, and a "parallel set" means - you guessed it - that the handles are about parallel to each other before you make your attempt). Now that rule was established in March 2004. So all certification after that happened according to the new rules.

You may still stumble across videos on the Internet with people demonstrating how to hold a gripper in your hand and doing it the Bill Piche way, or closing tough grippers with a parallel set. Remarkable feats in their own respect, but not ready for certification by IronMind®. This is why we will focus on credit card sets in our training. I'm not going to enter into a debate whether the new rules are fair or not, or what a "legitimate close" is and what not. Those on the list closed the grippers according to the rules then in effect, and hence have every right to be on that list. But the rules have changed, and now the grippers have to be closed according to the new rules. Period.

A few words on the **#4 and those certified for closing it**. It is no secret that all of those who officially certified for closing the #4 did so before March 2004. Those are Joe Kinney (1998), Nathan Holle, David Morton (both 2003), yes, also Tommy Heslep, and Magnus Samuelsson, the Swedish strongman (both 2004). Obviously, this has caused many to debate whether these guys are strong or not. Well, although I haven't met or talked to all of them personally, I dare say they are mind-blowingly strong. But it has also caused countless debates whether they are the only ones that are strong. There are guys who have closed the #4 according to the "old rules", but missed certification because the new rules were already in effect. Others claim to know someone whose brother has a cousin whose uncle has closed it the

---

[2] http://www.IronMind.com/IronMind/opencms/Main/captainsofcrush5.html#Rules_for_Closing. 16 January 2012.

first time he tried. But he didn't certify because he didn't bother. There is also a list of guys who have officially unofficially closed it. As paradox as it sounds, these are certainly guys who have a strong grip as well.

But let's not get too hung up about it. In fact, you can spend days browsing grip forums in search for answers to such questions. But is it going to get you anywhere? I think not. Is it going to get you anywhere to comment on YouTube videos with half-wisdoms and then let five guys show you they are cleverer? I have my doubts. Is it going to get you anywhere to **focus on your grip strength training** and how you can get the most out of it? I would go for this one.

Have any women ever certified for closing one of the grippers? Yes. Since 2011, women can certify for closing the #2. Adriane Blewitt was the first to do so. So there is a goal for you ladies.

A last word on why some think the new rules are unfair: they argue that people with small (meaning short) hands have **less of a chance of closing them** because of the credit card rule. This is another debate I don't want to enter, I'm just mentioning it on the side so that you are informed and can evaluate how your hand size might influence your achievements with the Captains of Crush® Grippers. Now, if your hands are too small, way below average, this would make it quite difficult for you to close a gripper with a credit card set - obviously. But, as Tommy tells me, if your hands are too large, it can be a disadvantage as well! (For closing the grippers, that is. For thick bar feats, obviously, the larger your hand, the better.) Tommy's right hand measures 7.5 inches (c. 19 cm). Joe Kinney's hands aren't that large. The hands of Gabriel Sum, official #3.5 closer and a freakish strong German boy, are 8.25 inches (c. 21 cm).

The bottom line is: the hands of great grip strength athletes seem to be **just about average**. Tommy's are even on the smaller side. He says if your hands are small, just "Work harder. It's possible." (Again, we are aware that when Tommy certified it was still according to the old rules, but remember: he has been seen closing the #3 with a no-set close quite easily since then.) **To measure the size of your hand** for comparison, lay a ruler across your open hand and measure the distance from the first wrist line to the top of the middle finger. Mine are 7.5 inches as well, for an example.

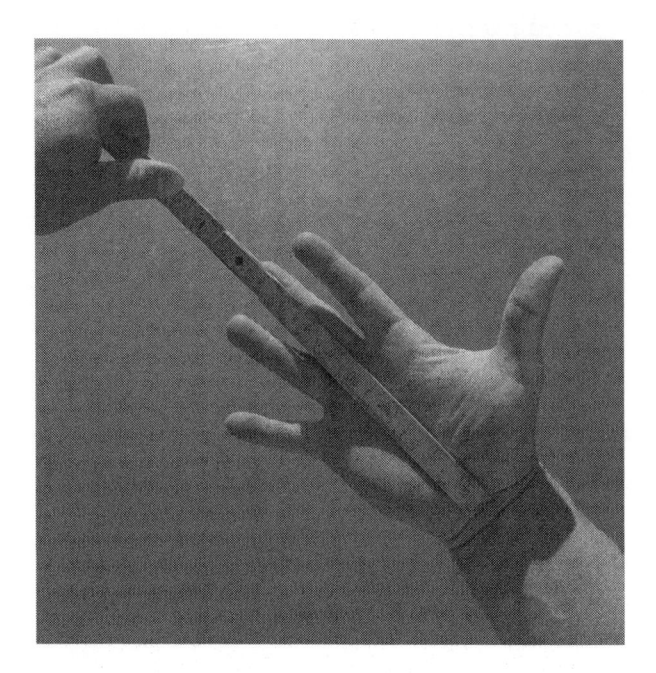

Fig. 4.1 Measuring the hand. In this case, 19cm, which is 7.5 inches

Another mystery surrounding the grippers is whether they are really thoroughly calibrated and whether grippers of the supposedly same difficulty nevertheless **vary in width** (meaning the distance between the handles from the outset) **and resistance** (meaning the amount of force required to close them) to a certain amount. IronMind® has quite a few words to say about this at: http://captainsofcrushgrippers.com/ironmind/opencms/gripperfact.html.
Read through that webpage before you form an opinion about it. Fact is, IronMind® introduced new types of springs on the grippers just a few years ago, which apparently "raised the bar in precision, durability and appearance."[3] Does that imply that the old springs were less precise? Probably. When comparing his own to other grippers, Tommy realized that his (old) #3 was one of the widest and hardest there is. But now that they have the new springs, we may assume that this problem is more or less eradicated. Let's decide this in their favour for now.

The last thing I could mention - but probably shouldn't really - is the infamous **dog leg**. If you look closely at you gripper, you realize that one of the ends of the spring is slightly more curved and the other is straighter before it coils into the spring. Some say you should pay attention to this when setting

---
[3] http://www.captainsofcrushgrippers.com/ 19 January 2012

the gripper in your hand, as one of the ends should be there or there, and the other one there, so that the gripper is easier to close. Tommy never noticed any difference, and IronMind® vehemently deny that there is one. If it does make a difference, it can only be minimal, or psychological at best, so let's disregard it for simplicity.

To learn more about the mysteries surrounding the Captain-of-Crush grippers, go to:
http://captainsofcrushgrippers.com/ironmind/opencms/gripperfact.html.

But get back to your training afterwards.

Summary

- In March 2004, the rules of closing the Captains of Crush® Grippers changed significantly. Since then, the handles of the grippers have to be credit-card-width apart before an attempt to close the gripper. As this is the legitimate way to do it at present, we will focus on it in our training.
- To measure the length of your hands can give you some idea of your chances to become good at the grippers. If your hands aren't below average, there is no hindrance to excel.
- Lots of mysteries surround the grippers. You can read about them on the IronMind® website, but we suggest you don't get too hung up about them.

4.2. How to Hold a Gripper Correctly

Here you will learn how to place the gripper in your hands in order to use your full power on them, and to avoid cheating at the same time.

If you have read the last chapter, you will know why it is crucial to learn how to set a gripper in your hand. **Instructions on the Internet can be misleading** in this regard, if they demonstrate how to do it legitimately according to the old rules.

That's why we will focus on the "**credit card set**" (CCS). It not only gives you a full range of motion for training, but, if you ever plan to certify on a gripper, it will prepare you from the start.

True, a "**no-set close**" (or "table no-set close" - closing the gripper without setting it at all and without any help from your other hand (what most laymen will try to perform the first time they try one of your grippers) - is an even fuller range of motion and more of a challenge. Occasionally you will want to try this for fun.

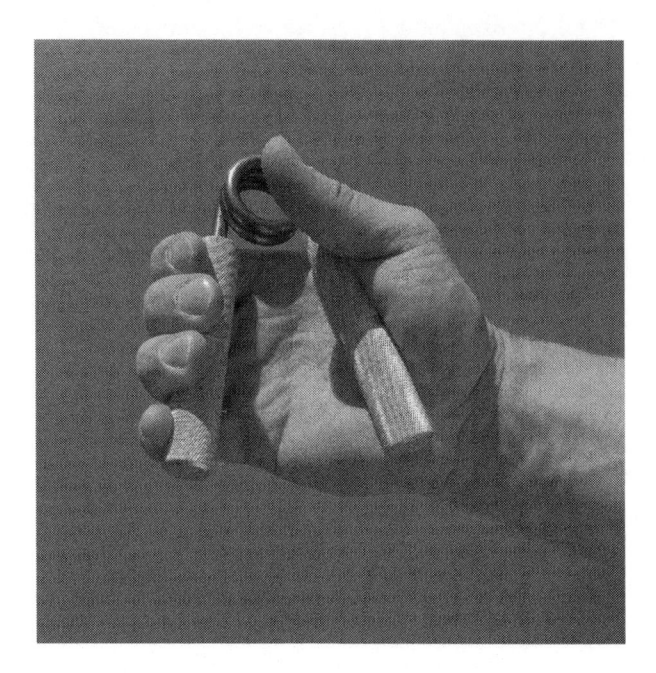

Fig. 4.2 A no-set, or "table no-set"

But a proper CCS has the **advantage** that you always perform your sets with the same preliminaries. It's just the best way to do it if you want to exert full power on your grippers and want to **measure your progress accurately**.

So here's how to do it (or one way to do it). Let's assume you want to close the gripper with your right hand:

a) Place one handle of the gripper firmly into about the centre of your right palm (spring upwards, of course), so that its lower end is at about the same level as an imagined line down from the tip of your pinky finger.
b) Keep it pressed into your palm with the thumb of your left hand so that it moves as little as possible, while you begin to partially close the gripper by pulling on the other handle with the index of your left hand. As you do so, begin to wrap the remaining fingers of your right hand around it to assist in this partial close.
c) Do so until the handles are about parallel to each other. Then let go with your left hand. In that position you should be able to hold the gripper with only your right hand quite firmly.

d) Quickly grab a credit card with your left hand. Hold it below the two gripper handles for measurement.
e) Slowly let the gripper open your right hand until you can slip the end of the credit card between the handles. Don't cheat!
f) Quickly remove the credit card.
g) Close the stupid little thing.

By practising, all of this should take you a few seconds at the most.

Grip Strength

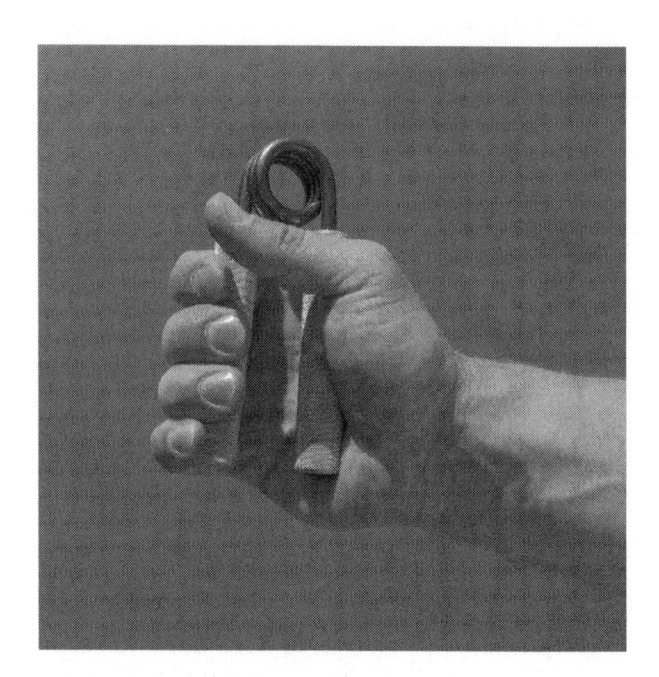

Fig. 4.3 For a CCS, start with a deep set...

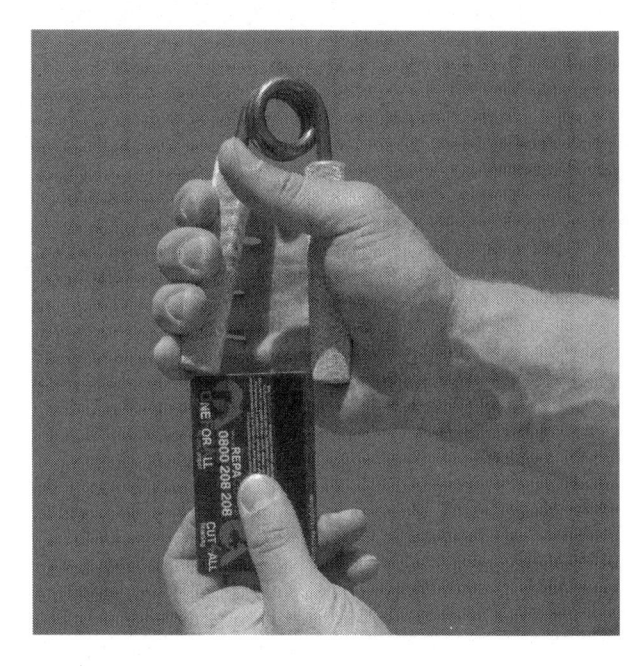

...let the gripper open gradually, until...

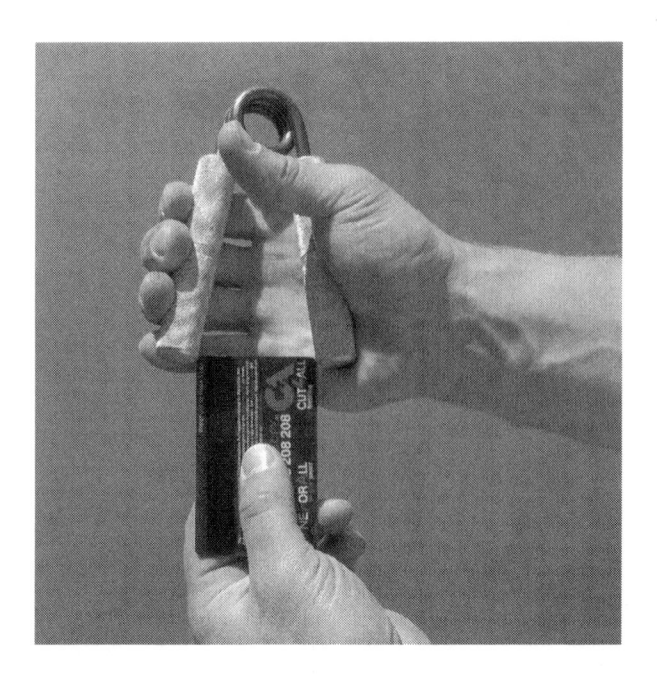

...a credit card fits between the handles...

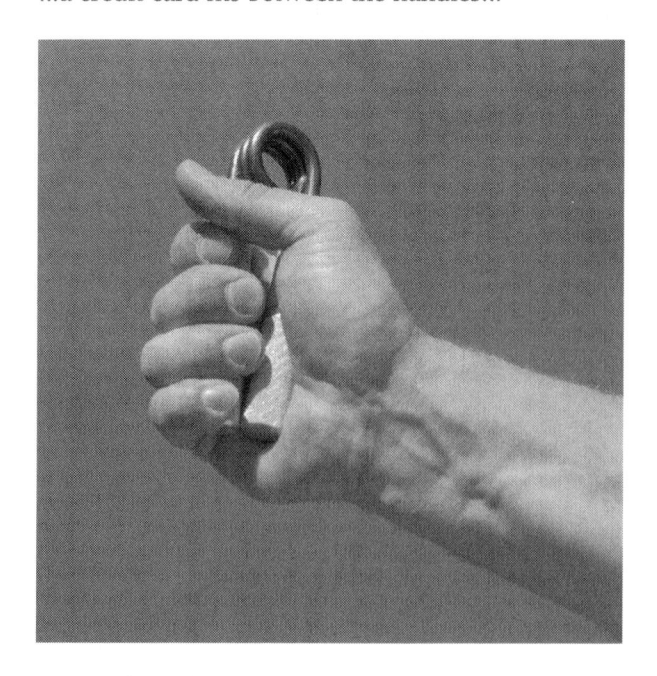

...then close the gripper!

Setting the gripper with a less-than-credit-card set first and then letting it open your hand will stretch your skin a bit, which will help you close your challenge gripper later, especially when you have small hands. It also makes you less dependent on chalk.

When doing reps, you don't necessarily have to check with a credit card whether the handles are properly apart after each rep. You could, for example, only check on the first rep, to make sure it is a proper credit card set, and then simply go by feeling on the reps following after, which will probably be not-quite-credit-card-sets. However, I prefer to check with a credit card before *each* rep. This is considerably harder than the first method, not at last because the set takes a little more time. But again, by this method I make sure to exercise the full range of motion with each rep.

You will realize that the anatomy of your hand is again decisive when it comes to setting the gripper in your hand. The size of the bulging muscles beneath your thumb (which actually move your thumb) and that of the muscles at the edge of your hand, beneath your pinky finger, can decide whether the gripper handle will slip out of your palm or not. This is only one of the reasons why you should train your thumb and all the other muscles in your hand as well. If those muscles are well developed and large, you will have an advantage in closing heavy grippers.

If you have never heard of anything like "setting" a gripper before and unconsciously used a "no-set" until now, you will quickly realize how much easier it is to close a gripper with the method prescribed here. Your challenge gripper will suddenly seem less out of reach.

Hint:
There is another way of setting a gripper which is considered an exercise in its own right: a "mash monster set" (MMS). When you set a gripper in your hand with the handles very close together, less than parallel, you are using an MMS. Doing reps with this set and never letting the handles open further than the initial position will allow you to do a great number of reps with a particular gripper, say, about three times as many as with a CCS. This exercise is helpful to become stronger on the very last momentum of the gripper close.

Summary

- Always aim for a CCS (Credit Card Set) when training with the grippers.
- Make sure that the one handle of the gripper is well embedded in your palm. Set the gripper in your one hand with the help of the other, closing it to less than a credit-card-width-distance between the handle. Let go with the assisting hand and let the gripper open the hand until its handles are credit-card-width apart. Then close it.
- When doing several reps, you may choose whether only your first rep is a credit card set, or all of them.
- Developing the muscles in your lower hand can help you in preventing a set gripper from slipping from your hand.

4.3. Training with Grippers: Exercises

Now let's cover a few basic gripper exercises and why you should try them.

The first and most basic exercise is **reps with the gripper** itself. Not much to add here. You know how to set it in your hand now. A full rep means you squeeze the handles together until they touch. You don't necessarily have to let it open up until CCS after each rep, as explained above, but you have to close it until the handles touch – otherwise it can't be considered a rep. Don't cheat! You are only cheating yourself.

Sometimes, especially during your last few really tough reps, it may happen that you are not sure whether the handles did touch or not. In such a case, the gripper has the benefit of the doubt, not you. Be true to yourself and only count those reps where you are sure the handles touched. An indication is the little clicking sound the handles make when they touch. Rely on it if you have no visual proof that the gripper closes, for example if your fingers block the view. But never count a full rep as a rep if you aren't 100% sure the gripper handles touched, because it will give you the illusion of progress where there is none. You can also ask a friend or training partner to check whether the handles touched.

Now. Of course, you would assume that to get better on closing the grippers, you would do just that: closing them. That is, using a lighter gripper for several reps and hoping that one day you will be able to close a harder gripper for one rep.

To get better on your bench press, you bench press, right?

True. You have to do the exercise you want to get better at. And you have to progressively overload: every once in a while you increase the resistance or do a rep more.

But how many gym rats do you know who vigorously perform their bench press every time they step into the weight room, but aren't getting anywhere since years? Compare that to the top powerlifters. How many of them do only squat, bench press, and deadlift nowadays? Usually they would do lots of assisting exercises, involving short-range movements, pauses, weird machinery, rubber bands, chains, boards, boxes, front squats, close-grip bench press, etc.

And you should try something similar in your grip strength training. Doing various gripper-related exercises besides the regular reps can really propel you forward. There are two ideas behind this:

A) Assisting exercises can target specific muscles or muscle groups which are the **weak link** in your grip. Let's say it is your pinky finger: it's so weak that it never does any work when you regularly try to close a gripper. Hence it's never stimulated and doesn't get stronger. But if it *was* stronger, it could assist in closing the gripper and your overall grip would be stronger.

B) Variation in itself is a benefit, because it makes your muscles face **new impulses**. If you know just a little bit about strength training or bodybuilding you should know about this as well. Your muscles get stronger because they adapt to new challenges. Once they have adapted, they don't grow bigger or stronger. That's why you can't make progress following the same routine for years and years. Your body adapts to it and stops to grow. If you try new exercises, however, or a different rep-set scheme, there is a new stimulus, and you'll get stronger in the attempt to adapt.[4]

Naturally, you can make great progress for several weeks if you just started your grip strength training with the heavy duty grippers. You will do regular reps over and over again, and soon the number of reps you can do will increase. At one point, however, progress will just stop and you will wonder what is happening. After some more weeks of trying you will probably tell yourself: "well, that's the best I can do, apparently I can't get any stronger than that" (quietly adding: "anyone who can do better must be using steroids"[5]).

That's one thing you can do. Or you can try some new exercises:

1) Negatives
A highly effective exercise you shouldn't miss. Take a gripper you can't close, like your challenge gripper (some even use a gripper one step above their challenge gripper). Set it in your hand, then **force** it shut. Tommy does that with the help of his other hand in front of his chest (Alternatively, you can push it against your thigh or hip until it's closed, without the help of the other hand). Then let go with the other hand, and, as the gripper forces your hand open, fight the resistance as much as you can. You should get to a point where you can just hold the gripper shut for about four or five seconds, then slowly let it open your hand. In the beginning, of course, you won't be able to do that: just fight it for 4 to 5 second, then let it open very slowly. You will get better in time.

By the way, when we say "fight it", we mean it. Don't just think "wow, this is tough" and slowly open your hand. That's not a negative. Fight against

---
[4] Another idea behind some of the assisting exercises powerlifters perform is, of course, the supporting equipment used in powerlifting nowadays.
[5] Which isn't true, by the way.

your hand opening as if your life would depend on it. This is how you get stronger. This is crucial.

Ask any sport scientist about the effectiveness of negatives in strength training. They usually swear by them.

2) Strap holds

This is one of the exercises invented by John Brookfield and now widely used. We have described it above in the equipment section. You loop a thin piece of strap through the centre of a weight plate and squeeze the other end of the strap between the handles of a gripper you can close for some reps. The thinner the webbing, the more closed the gripper has to be. Then you lift the weight plate off the ground until it dangles from your gripper by the strap. Hold it as long as you can.

Quite tricky, isn't it? Don't worry, you will get used to it.

Mind you: this is a static exercise that trains your grip strength in the **very last range of motion of a gripper close** (that range where you are usually weakest). For the exercise to be most effective, I recommend you use a webbing as thin as possible. Even if you are able to handle more weight with a thicker strap, put the weight in second place (actually you should put it in third place, as we will see). Once you can handle a 1.25 lbs (c. 0.5 kg) barbell plate with a very thin strap, go on to increase the weight - but keep using the same strap (I hope it will hold - leather is a good idea).

Of course there is one more component in the exercise: the duration of holding it. If you do grip strength training to assist you in your primary sport, be that climbing, judo, wrestling, or, who knows, strongman, you might decide for yourself that endurance is most important to you. Then you can let a friend check with a stop watch for how long you can uphold that 1.25 lbs plate. Gradually, you should increase the duration in the course of your workouts, and every once in a while you might want to increase the weight. Durations of up to a minute shouldn't be uncommon, then.

If, however, your aim is closing a specific gripper, or simply maximum crushing grip strength for certain grip strength feats, you should aim to increase the weight whenever possible. Even if you uphold the weight for only a few seconds, you will benefit more than by going for endurance. Also, you should always aim to use the heaviest gripper with which you can do a strap hold at all. Actually, this should be your list of priorities:

a) Thinnest strap
b) Heaviest gripper

c) Heaviest weight
d) Duration

Just for the record, Tommy did strap holds with the CoC® #3 with up to 35 lbs (c. 15 kg). That's a *lot* of weight!

Once you have that weight dangling from the strap, you simply hold it for as long as you can, Tommy says. He adds: "You have to have your mind in the right place. And you don't wanna hold your breath. The more oxygen you get in there, the better your muscles work. Keep your mind set: 'I'm not gonna give up. I'm determined to do this. I don't care what people say. They tell me I'm too small and too weak, I'll show 'em. Just watch this.'"

3) Machine work

If you do have a machine which resembles the movement of the hand grippers, like a Gripanator, a floor model grip machine, or something home-made, you can use it in several ways, but **the best way to use them is for negatives also**. They are really effective. And a machine allows you to do them in a more precise way.

Let's have a look at how to exercise with your machine:

a) Once the machine is loaded, get a good grip on the handles, then shut them **with the help of the other hand**.
b) Machines have the advantage that they are - usually - much easier to close with the help of the other hand than it is to force a heavy gripper shut. So most likely you will have a chance to adjust your grip a little until comfortable.
c) Then **hold it fully closed** for as long as you can. (How long that is going to be depends on the weight you chose. Ideally, if you want to go for maximum strength, you choose one that allows you to hold it shut for a very short time - like a few seconds.)
d) When it gradually opens, let go and **repeat with other hand**, or force it shut again and **do another rep** (most people would alternate hands instead of doing several reps with one hand).

To find out how much weight you should load onto your machine, **just try until you find a weight you can barely handle** (don't cheat) and gradually aim to increase the weight. In the beginning, while you are getting used to the machine, don't load that much weight onto it until it doesn't even allow you to hold the machine shut for at least a second or so. If the weight is as heavy that it forces your hand open right away - so that you will only be able to hold it steady with the handles as little as only a few millimetres apart - the weight is too heavy to get used to the feeling of negatives. Remember: in the equipment section I talked about the ideal case that your machine allows training beyond the range. If that is the case, you don't want to shoot this advantage down by loading the machine with too much weight, so that it forces your hand open immediately.

But once you get used to the machine, and get used to really fighting it, you can also load it with so much weight that it opens your hands right away.

Actually, you can do two slightly different exercises in this way: You can do holds, meaning you go for a specific amount of time you hold the machine handles shut. Or you do pure negatives, meaning you use a heavier weight that hardly allows you to hold the handles shut. On his Gripanator, Tommy would do holds with about 100 lbs (c. 45 kg) loaded on the machine, and negatives with about 130 lbs (c. 59 kg). As the machine has a certain leverage, those 130 lbs equalled about 400 lbs (c. 181 kg) of pressure on his hands (that's stronger than the #4). In the latter case his hand would open right away. But he would fight it and "hang on for life".

To understand how important it is to really hold the machine handles shut and work on that last little part of the movement of closing a gripper when doing holds, consider this: The Gripanator has bolts which are optionally applied to the machine and put the handles real close together from the start, so they won't even open up beyond a certain range. It gives you the same feel as putting a choker on a regular gripper so it won't open fully (a common technique as well). That way you are forced to work on the last section of the movement, because once the handles of the machine open as far that they are stopped by the bolt, there isn't much left for you to do. You will really fight them handles so they won't touch the bolts!

For Tommy, however, the bolts that came with his Gripanator weren't long enough. They didn't put the handles close enough together. He really wanted to force himself to work on that very, very last section of the close. So he went to the hardware store and purchased a bolt which was long enough. He then did holds of 5 to 10 seconds at the most before his hand would slowly open. "It worked," he says.

If you want to do both holds and pure negatives in one workout, you can (after you have warmed up properly) load the machine with a heavy weight and do a few sets of negatives. Then you reduce the weight and perform a few holds. Doing the two exercises in this order makes sure that your hands are still fresh when you do the heavy negatives, so that you can use full power on this more difficult exercise.

> **Hint:**
> You have probably realized how much your grip strength training can benefit from innovation, improvisation, and experimentation. Don't be afraid to try things out. Your equipment is there to suit you, not the other way round. Maybe you will come up with your own, home-made grip strength machine. In any case, be prepared to become a more frequent visitor of your local hardware store. It might not be a bad idea to befriend the sales clerk. He will help you out wherever he can and give you advice to get you the things you need. Remember: making or adjusting your training equipment with your own hands not only saves you money but can be a lot of fun too.

I mentioned that you might have the possibility to adjust your grip on the machine until comfortable, in contrast to a heavy gripper you have to force shut for negatives. That's a tricky one, because the grip that is most comfortable and allows you to hold the weight for the longest time might not be the most effective one. Usually, if you close the machine handles, you would wrap your finger around them as tight as possible and hold. But now imagine closing a gripper with a credit card set. Your finger might not be completely wrapped around it at the end of the movement. You will rather notice that some of the strength comes from the part of the fingers closer to the finger tips instead of closer to the palm. It is not actually the ideal position to hold the gripper shut (that's why people invented the parallel and deep set). Still, those are the rules and that's how you have to do it. So you have to train for it. Meaning that, when working with a machine, you ideally hold the handles of the machine shut like you would hold a gripper shut after a credit card set. This position varies from person to person as everybody has differently-sized hands. So observe and experiment.

If this sounds to scientific, just forget about it. Machine work will do its part either way.

By the way, I mentioned it before: you can also use a regular gripper for beyond the range training if you **grind off the handles** at the bottom, so that they can be moved closer together. Here, the same applies as for any machine work. Obviously, you would use a slightly lighter gripper. For example, if you can just barely close a #2, you could use a #1.5.

I don't have to tell you about the **disadvantages** of this method: By manipulating the gripper you risk damaging it and hurting yourself. You are generally apt to squeeze your skin when closing such a manipulated gripper. You cannot adjust the resistance in small steps, and as you grow stronger, your one manipulated gripper becomes useless and you have to "damage" another one. You cannot close it with the help of you other hand as comfortably as you could close a machine.

The **advantages** are: it's easier to carry a manipulated gripper around with you than a cumbersome machine. In all likelihood, another gripper is easier to obtain and cheaper than a grip machine (unless you build one yourself). And, training with a gripper with ground off handles comes closest to training with a regular gripper.

4) Gripper upside down

Now here is a nice exercise if you get bored of doing the same exercises over and over again: simply place a moderate gripper in your hand with the spring down and the ends of the handles up. To be able to close a gripper in this manner you will probably have to set it considerably with your other hand. You will also be less strong than with regular closes. If you usually do reps with the #2, try a #1 or #1.5 for this exercise.

I need not say this exercise is most effective if you aim for a close of the gripper you are holding upside down. It's tough, but it feels good for a change. Remember, any variation in your training every once in a while is a good thing, as it confronts your muscles with new impulses.

So if you aren't getting ahead any more, if you feel stuck, include this exercise in your routine for a couple of weeks and hopefully it will make a change.

5) Isolating fingers

The idea behind the following exercise is that some fingers on your hand are stronger than the others (obviously), and hence, when you try to close a gripper with all four fingers, it's usually the stronger fingers (especially the middle finger) that do most of the work. As a consequence, they get more training impulses and become stronger faster than the other fingers. The difference in strength between the fingers increases. It's a vicious cycle.

So, to train specific fingers, you simply hold a lighter gripper in your hand in such a manner that not all of the fingers assist in closing it. For example, you could hold the gripper upside down and try to close it with your ring and pinky finger only (of course you can set it in you hand so that you can wrap your fingers around it comfortably). Obviously, you would need a rather light gripper in relation to your current challenge gripper for this.

The opposite, holding the gripper with the spring facing upwards, as usual, but placing it thus far up in your hand that only middle and index finger touch the handles, is also done quite often. Most of the time, this is performed as a feat of strength - "closing the gripper with two fingers only". Naturally, you would use the two strongest fingers in your hand for that: middle and index finger.

But I believe to boost strength gains in your hand it makes most sense to isolate your weaker fingers. As it can be quite awkward to try to close even a light gripper with your ring and pinky fingers, IronMind® has introduced the **IMTUG**™ grippers, small grippers with short handles, rounded off at the ends, and with less resistance than the regular grippers. You might want to check them out at the IronMind® store.

Now you have read about some basic assisting exercises with the grippers. There are lots and lots more you might come across, though. Even closing attempts on your challenge gripper can be considered exercises in their own right. Maybe you will even come up with a new exercise yourself. Just don't underestimate the positive effects such various exercises can have on your grip training and perform them regularly for a change.

Summary
- Besides doing regular reps with your gripper, it is wise to include alternative exercises. First, because they might target the weak link in your grip, second, because the variation offers new training impulses.
- Five of the most effective assisting exercises have been introduced here: negatives, strap holds, machine work, gripper upside down, isolating fingers.
- There are lots of other alternative exercises you might come across. Don't hesitate to try them out.

4.4. Training with Grippers: Reps and Sets
Here you will learn how many reps and sets of each exercise you should perform.

One of the most frequent questions aspiring grip athletes ask is, how many sets and reps should they perform?

Part of this question has already been answered indirectly here, but let's go about it in detail.

1) Reps
The whole idea behind heavy-duty grippers and why they were developed is because at some point it was time to reveal the fact that regular, plastic-handled hand grippers, available from any sporting goods store, are not that useful. You can easily squeeze out 500 reps with one of those, but it won't make you stronger. Your grip muscles react to training similarly as the muscles in the rest of your body. If you want to improve your bench press, you probably work with a maximum of 5, maybe 6 reps, and sometimes even perform singles.

This is how you develop maximum strength in all skeletal muscles, hand strength included.[6] Tommy **never went beyond 10 reps** in his regular grip strength training, because he knew that anything which would go far beyond that would build endurance, not maximum strength (of course, some of you might want to build endurance instead of, or in addition to, maximum strength, but let's focus on the latter for the moment). So you must train with reps in a scope between one and ten, preferably even less - let's say six - reps. Accordingly, you need a gripper which is so hard to close that you cannot possibly perform more complete reps than that. This would be the gripper for your working sets we talked about. As soon as you can do more than ten full reps with it, consider it a warm-up gripper and move on to the next one. If you can't close your challenge gripper yet, then you should probably move to one of the in-between grippers. Let's say your working gripper used to be the #2, and your challenge gripper the #3. You can do more than 10 reps with the #2, but can't close the #3 yet. Then a #2.5 is probably a good choice, as you will, in all likelihood, be able to close it at least once, maybe three times, or more. Else, if you can't afford another gripper, you might want to resort to negatives with the #3 and other exercises.

So much for regular reps with the grippers. The same applies to all other exercises with repetitive movements, like training with the gripper upside down, or isolating fingers.

---

[6] The matter is a bit more complex, and there are other ways, but in general this is the basic method.

As to static exercises like negatives, strap holds, and machine work, it's best to consider one set as one rep in which you give everything. It just shouldn't last too long. A strap hold should be so difficult that you can hold it for a few seconds only, let's say not much more than ten. The same applies to holds with a machine. Also negatives with grippers or a machine shouldn't take forever.

But don't get us wrong: don't simply release the hold because you're above ten seconds. And don't open your hand faster when doing negatives in fear it will take longer than it should. As I quoted Tommy above, hang on for life doing these exercises. If it takes too long this time, so be it. Keep track and increase the resistance next time!

2) Sets

How many sets of each exercise should one perform, and of how many sets should a complete grip strength workout consist?

This is a tricky question.

Some say three intense sets is enough, preferably you should even do only one set but put all your energy into it. Others do endless sets.

Tommy, for example, (although he never counted or kept track), remembers doing lots of sets (but he also says he did too much at times). One of his gripper workouts during an early stage, before he could close the #3, would have looked like this (this is just an instructive example, we will give you more sample routines later):

Gripper	Exercise	Sets	Reps	Note
Trainer	Regular reps	1	10	Warm-up
#1	Regular reps	1	10	Warm-up
#2	Regular reps	1	10	Warm-up
#3	Closing attempts	3-4	1	
#3	Negatives	20-30	1	Forced close with help of other hand

The routine above would be followed by pinch grip training, etc. You probably noticed the great number of negative sets: 20-30. Tommy himself told me that this was probably too much. He suggests five sets of negatives should be enough. Again: "get in, hit it hard, and get out" is probably the better way for most people than endless sets.

The key is **intensity**. If you can really put everything into one single set per exercise, do it. For most, however, this is difficult, as one tends to hold something back. So a number of intense sets somewhere between two and five per exercise seems most reasonable for the majority of aspiring grip strength athletes. You will agree that it becomes difficult to uphold maximum intensity for much more than five sets.

But it's not rocket science: After a proper warm-up, I'd say with any combination of **2-5 exercises, with 1-5 sets and 1-8 reps** for each (depending on the exercise - remember that negatives are always singles) you can't do much wrong.

Just don't forget that everybody's different and feel free to experiment until you find what works best for you. For some, the minimum will suffice, for others, the maximum will not be enough and they will decide to do even a few more sets on their favourite exercise. Others, whose hands are used to hard work, will perhaps make fast progress with over 20 sets - maybe they need a few sets more to build up intensity in the course of their workout and/or they have the mental strength to keep up the intensity through that many sets! (We have included a sample routine for this kind of person below.)

As long as you go for maximum intensity, as long as you make progress, and as long as you recover from each workout, you are on the right path.

Summary

- On dynamic exercises like regular reps with a gripper, or with the gripper upside down, to increase strength, choose a gripper which will allow you to do no more than ten reps.
- For static exercises like strap holds, and for negatives, consider one rep one set. Choose a resistance which ensures you hold the tension for not too long.
- It is recommended to perform between 2 and 5 sets per exercise. If, however, you feel able to put all your energy into one set, this might suffice. If your hands can take it, there is practically no limit to the number of sets you perform.
- Ultimately, you will have to experiment until you find out what works best for you, that is, which combination of sets and reps allows you to recover between workouts, but provides ample strength gains.
- Intensity matters more than quantity.

Hint:

A strong crushing grip is especially useful for powerlifters, strongmen, martial arts which use a gi (like Judo or Brasilian Jiu-Jitsu), and no-gi grappling-based martial arts, including MMA.

5. PINCH GRIP

In this chapter you will learn what a pinch grip is and why it is wise to develop a strong pinch grip. You will also be introduced to a few pinch grip exercises and sets-and-reps schemes will be suggested.

Now that you have learned about proper crushing grip training, it's time to cover training for another type of grip strength: the pinch grip. What differentiates the pinch grip from the crushing grip is that it is a **static kind of strength**, that it involves a lot of **strength from your thumbs**, and that you cannot develop as much strength as in the crushing grip, because of the awkward leverage. The latter fact might be the reason why pinch grip training enjoys much less popularity than gripper training. But if you try it out for a while, you will in all likelihood discover how many fun things you can do with a strong pinch grip, and how helpful it can be in everyday life. You will develop a consciousness for how often you make use of your pinch grip during the day, and how comfortable it would be to be able to lift 90 lbs (c. 40 kg) squeezed between your finger tips and thumb. Not all everyday objects have handles where you can apply your crushing grip. Furniture, boards, books, weight plates, tiles, bricks, laptops, etc. will frequently stress your pinch grip. Moreover, lots of nice grip feats exist which allow you to test and rank your pinch grip easily. It is also quite easy to train this kind of grip strength with cheap, everyday objects. You should definitely give it a try.

Fortunately, pinch grip training is less of a science than gripper training. If you go for maximum strength rather than endurance, there is only one parameter of variation, and that is the thickness of the object you lift, i.e. the distance between your fingers and thumb, or how wide you have to spread your hand apart, as you perform the lift. You should train both with objects of little thickness, and with rather thick ones, and you can train with flat, rectangular objects, like a weighted board or four-by-four, and with round objects, like the hub of a York barbell plate or a "blob" (the weight of one side of a one-piece dumbbell cut off).

Two aspects of hand strength are particularly stressed in pinch grip training, which are only secondary in gripper training: **the thumb and the fingertips**. This is why pinch grip training is the ideal and necessary supplement to your gripper training, in order for you to work on all aspects of your grip strength.

Especially the thumb is the weak link, and if you have been training your crushing grip for a considerable amount of time but never cared about pinch grip training, you will notice how measly your accomplishments will be there, as you miss the strength from your thumbs. Therefore, start training your pinch grip right away, so it will measure up to your crushing grip. It's going to be fun.

5.1. Pinch Grip: Exercises
A taste of the many pinch grip exercises out there.

There are countless movements which challenge your pinch grip, and every day people find new ones. We will explain a few basic ones to you. We will also introduce some thumb specific exercises to strengthen this weak link.

> **Hint:**
>
> **Occasionally, I speak of a four- three- or two-finger pinch grip etc. This is not counting the thumb. A two-finger pinch grip means lifting an object pinched between thumb on the one side and index- and middle finger on the other side of the object, for example.**

1) Pinching wooden blocks

Now it's time to talk about training with the wooden blocks we introduced in the equipment section. Actually, they are pretty self-explanatory. Just hook a weight to the cable, grab the wooden block - whether the thinner or the thicker one - so that as much skin of your hand as possible is in contact with the block. Push your finger downwards so that the **band of skin between your index and thumb touches the block**. You might find it helpful to touch the block with your thumb first, low down, and then "wrap" the rest of you fingers around.

Again, as this is a static exercise, like strap holds with a gripper, or holds with a grip machine, go for as much resistance as possible, while not necessarily going for duration with a lighter weight. If you want to train endurance, that's fine, but if you want to gain strength, conquer heavier weights, and do feats of grip strength, use as much weight as possible, even if you can hold it for only a very short time. If you have managed a certain weight and can hold it successfully for several seconds, keep track and increase the weight next time. This is the advantage of using wooden blocks with a cable - you can increase the weight gradually by small steps if you have plenty of weight plates at hand (if you haven't, don't worry - you can always use buckets of water, sand, or stones instead, which is what Tommy did in the beginning).

If you want to **target specific fingers**, for similar reasons as explained in the crushing grip exercises section, this is what you can do: you can pinch the wooden block with all fingers except the pinky, or with only middle and index finger. To do this, the remaining finger(s), in that case the pinky, or the pinky and the ring finger, are NOT simply spread away from your hand. This would be a feat of hand and finger coordination in itself and rob you of much of your concentration. It would also tempt you to instinctively put these fingers on the object and mess up your set. Instead, curl the finger(s) you don't want to use into your hand, as you would when making a fist.

If you want to isolate your ring and pinky finger only, which is something you should definitely try sometime, use a different technique: Put your middle and index finger on the upper side of the block, where the band between thumb and index touched the block up until now. If you are holding the object on your side, your middle and index finger are now pointing forward. This is the most comfortable way to pinch grip without your index and middle finger. You will not be able to lift a lot of weight in this manner.

Most of the time, however, you should train with all four fingers opposite the thumb, as you want your thumb to be the weak link. This way it is stressed most in training and grows stronger, while your fingers get ample training through your crushing grip workouts anyway.

2) Pinching barbell plates (rim)

This is basically the same exercise as pinching wooden blocks, but it is more of a challenge. It is more difficult because the plates sometimes tend to slide apart, and it is more challenging because the plates don't allow as much variation when it comes to resistance. On the other hand, specific plates are benchmarks of pinch grip strength which allow you to compare your achievements to accomplished grip strength athletes. For instance, pinching and lifting two 45 lbs (c. 20 kg) barbell plates with a standard width of about 1.25 - 1.5 inch (3-4 cm) is a remarkable feat of pinch grip strength. Tommy lifted two 45s in this manner with index and middle finger only, by the way.

Fig. 5.1 Tommy pinching two 45 lbs plates with thumb, index, and middle finger only (unfortunately, only a camera phone was at hand when this happened)

If you want to work towards **pinch lifting two 45s**, but aren't strong enough to do this yet, there are **two ways** to go. The **first** is probably the better way, but it requires additional equipment - a simple iron pipe with a 2 inch (c. 50 mm) diameter and, let's say at least 12 inch (c. 30 cm) in length (you can use the same tool for thick bar training, by the way. In that case you might want to go for a slightly longer pipe. See equipment section). Make sure you have collars which fit on the pipe. The idea is that you can load it with your barbell plates like a barbell without a handle, and fix the weights with collars so they won't come off. (If you are using barbell plates with a narrower drilling, use an accordingly thinner pipe instead.) Then, load two 45s onto this pipe, with smooth sides out, as you would normally pinch them. Try to pinch and lift these with *two hands* for a test (a proper lift would be to grab it and stand up with it, at least until you are upright with hips and legs straight, as in a deadlift). If you have a fairly strong grip you will be able to do so (if not, work towards it with lesser plates or wooden blocks). Now, to work from lifting two 45s with two hands to lifting them with one hand, load barbell plates onto the pipe on both sides of the two 45s equally, and fix them with the collars. Always lift with a two-hand pinch grip. Now you have a comfortable tool which you can load with weight plates, increasing the resistance in small steps as you grow stronger, while you can always apply the same grip (Obviously, you need to load it with plates with a smaller overall diameter than the two 45s in the center so you will be able to apply the same grip). Note that lifting the weight of four 45s in this manner does not necessarily mean you have the strength to lift two 45s with one hand, which is considerably more difficult, as the plates are not connected in any way - other than in the method just described.

Fig. 5.2 Pinching barbell plates with an iron pipe and two collars

As mentioned, the **second** way requires less equipment, but is also less effective. Simply put two 45's together, again with the smooth sides out, and, if lifting them with both hands is too easy, lift it with one full hand and only three or two finger of the other hand. For the next set, switch hands: Let's say you started with your full right hand in the first set. Now use all fingers of the left hand and three or two of the right hand to assist, always applying a proper pinch grip with both hands as you just learned, including the "isolating fingers pinch grip".

As you grow stronger, the assisting hand should do less and less work. If you start with a three-finger pinch on the assisting hand, work towards a two-finger pinch, eventually assisting with thumb and index only. Then proceed to loosen the pinch grip of the assisting hand from its "optimum" to a somewhat weaker hold, for example by not touching the plates with the skin between index and thumb. Carry on in this manner until the assisting hand does very little work. In the end, you will hopefully be able to lift the two 45s completely without the assisting hand and with one hand only!

Once you have this feat managed, you can work towards lifting them with a three-finger pinch of one hand only, or add weight in the same manner as described above, with an iron pipe on which you put barbell plates.

Now this is one way to train your pinch grip with barbell plates, but there is another, which stresses your "**open hand**" pinch grip strength. This means that you use lighter and smaller barbell plates, but several of them, so that the object you pinch is much wider. Obviously, this is much more difficult, and you won't be able to handle as much weight as when pinching two plates only. You can use a stack of 5 lbs (c. 2.5 kg) plates, or try 10 lbs (c. 5 kg) plates (not easy). Just make sure you use the right ones: preferably without plastic or rubber coating, a smooth outside, no 'round' edges, and all of the same size. The hardest part of this will be to avoid the inside plates from slipping out, as the plates will tend to fan out at the bottom. Give it a try if your gym has enough plates of the same size and add plates as you grow stronger. If you aren't making progress, try to connect the plates to each other to make it easier, either by a pipe, in the same way as described above, or with short pieces of rope, wire, a rubber band, or anything you can find. If might suffice to do this simply to keep them from fanning out.

3) Pinching barbell plates (hub)

Lifting a deep-dish barbell plate by the hub is another notorious feat of grip strength and puts yet another, slightly different stress on your grip muscles. It's also considered a pinch grip feat and requires a lot of strength from your thumb and fingertips. Strong guys can do this with a 45 lbs (c. 20 kg) plate.

The most difficult thing here will be to find the right plates in the first place. The traditional York barbell plates are frequently used, but not every gym has them (or comparable ones). Chances are that the plates in your gym have either no hub at all, or that the hub is too wide or not deep enough. In this case a home-made device will offer remedy. In the simplest form, this will be a short piece of iron pipe, around 3 inches (c. 7.6 cm) in diameter, with a collar at the bottom with two holes to fit a cable through. Weights can be attached to the cable. Instead of an iron pipe you can also use wood. Obviously, such a simple device can not offer the exact same effect as lifting an actual barbell plate from the floor, but you will certainly work the muscles required for such a feat. If you work your way up with a home-made device and one day a friend challenges you with a York barbell plate, you will probably be able to impress him. If you don't want to build your own device, there is also the IronMind® Hub-Style Pinch Gripper, which can be used to train this kind of pinch grip feat with variable resistance by adding weight to it with a cable or loading pin.

4) Pinching blobs

That your gym is equipped with "blobs" is even less likely. Those are cylindrical weights **sawed off from a one-piece metal dumbbell**, or preserved in singularity. Most wanted are such from traditional York barbell company dumbbells. Lifting the end weight of a 100 lbs (c. 45 kg) dumbbell, weighing a little less than 50 lbs (c. 22.5 kg) in one of the ways described in the following is a nice feat of hand strength. Of course, if you can find a dumbbell constructed in a similar way, it doesn't have to be a York one, and you can also use hexagonal ones. There are also companies who manufacture blobs solely for the purpose of grip strength training, in various formats. Their advantage is that they are a fixed weight you can play around with and test your pure strength, rather than dexterity, as you don't have to worry it will fall apart, as weight plates would do if you wouldn't take care. A blob also offers a variety of training possibilities in one tool.

If you cannot find blobs, there is always the possibility to make you own training device out of wood (with a hole or hook to fit a cable through and to add weight plates), but it will be less fun to lift and not look as good as an "original" blob.

Here are some ways to lift a blob:

Starting with the easiest, you simply pinch the blob between your thumb and four fingers, each on one of the "flat" sides. I put "flat" in inverted commas, because most blobs have a slight curvature, on either one side, on both sides equally, or on both sides but to a different degree. Of course, depending on how your blob is shaped, it will make it more or less difficult to be lifted, depending on where you put your fingers and thumb. Experiment.

Next you can try the same with less than four fingers. In the same manner as described above in the context of weight plate pinching, you can lift, for example, with thumb, index, and middle finger only, or with thumb, ring, and pinky finger only.

Now, for open hand pinch grip training, lay the blob on the floor on one of the "flat" sides. Then spread your fingers across it while pushing down on it, grab it as if you had eagle claws, and lift it. This is probably the most difficult way to lift a blob.

5) Thumb machine/Jewel

Now that you have learned about methods to both train and test your pinch grip directly, I also want to introduce you to a way to catapult your pinch grip to new heights indirectly.

As explained above, the thing about the pinch grip is that it involves a lot of strength from your thumb. In many pinch grip feats, your thumb is directly opposed to your four fingers, meaning it is expected to do the same work as four fingers, but on its own. This is why your thumb will be the weak link most of the time. And as you train your four fingers to become stronger and stronger by closed-hand crushing grip training, your thumb is having a hard time to catch up. Now, by **targeting the thumb alone**, you can level out this imbalance to a certain degree. Ideally, you should do this **with a dynamic movement** to complement your static pinch grip training and train your thumb muscles across a full range of motion at the same time.

Unfortunately, there aren't that many methods to do this effectively.

Probably the best by far is a thumb machine. Like the Titan's Telegraph Key™ available from IronMind®. But they are rather expensive. Here is one I built on my own:

Fig. 5.3 A home-made thumb machine

Training with it is pretty self-explanatory. Find out what amount of weight is right for you to start with, and then work your way up progressively. The most straightforward way to work with it is by performing reps as you would with any machine or barbell exercise. Note that although you want to build maximum strength primarily, performing anywhere between 2 and 6 reps per set, you may also want to perform higher reps from time to time, let's say between 8 and 15, aiming for hypertrophy (muscle growth): because a larger thumb pad muscle will help you with the training on the grippers by keeping the gripper handle in your palm from sliding towards your wrist.

Of course you can also do holds with a telegraph-key machine. But remember that most of your pinch grip training will be static anyway, so I suggest you make use of the opportunity for some dynamic training.

Another effective way of training your thumbs with such a machine are **negatives**. For these you would load the machine with a heavy weight which you can nevertheless lift (or "press down") with both hands/thumbs. Once you have pressed it all the way down, let go with one hand/thumb, an thus perform a negative on the other, trying to resist the weight as much as possible as it forces your hands to open up. Then switch sides. Repeat. (Note that a negative with one thumb - with a weight which you can barely lift with two thumbs - will be very tough to do.)

There are three ways to exercise your thumb on such a machine (there might be others, but those are the most important ones). That is, three ways of holding the handles:

A) The first one is the most natural one which gives you the best leverage. Imagine curling your fingers, especially your index finger, inward as you would when making a fist. Hold your hands vertically in front of the machine, thumbs pointing upwards. Then press you index fingers against the lower, immobile part of the handle. With your thumbs, catch the upper, moving part of the handle. Then push downwards with your thumbs to lift the weight up. I recommend this style for most of the exercises, as it is the least awkward one and gives you the opportunity to work your thumbs with the least distraction.

B) The second way closely resembles a regular pinch grip. Here you push all four fingertips of your straightened fingers against the lower bar while pushing downwards on the moving handle with your thumbs. It's basically like a dynamic pinch grip. The advantage is, of course, that it prepares you ideally for heavy pinch grip feats. The downside of this method is that it might feel a bit awkward to get into the position for it, which could distract you from your work on heavy weights.

C) The third method is simply the reverse of method B). The tips of your thumbs push against the lower bar, while your four finger tips push against the moving handle and press it downwards. This is the least recommended method, as it requires mostly static strength from your thumb, while your fingers do the major dynamic part. You can try it for a change, though.

In the equipment section we already mentioned a simple, home-made device for effective thumb training developed by Tommy Heslep himself, which he called the **Jewel**. Originally, Tommy developed this tool with the help of his father to work on the specific grip required for the feat of tearing decks of cards. But it can also be used in a very similar way to a thumb machine, being much cheaper and easily made.

Of course, the springs on the jewel have a different dynamic than a plate-loaded thumb machine, but remember that the grippers are spring-based as well and still considered the most effective grip strength tool.

To work your thumb on the jewel, grab it with both hands on two opposing sides (if yours is rectangular, like Tommy's, grab the longer edges). Now you can apply the same grip variations as on the thumb machine, either with curled index finger pressing against the bottom, or with all four fingertips on either the top or the bottom, like in a pinch grip (I recommend the first variation). Negatives and holds are possible, as with a thumb machine, but the most straightforward way to make use of the jewel will be dynamic reps.

To be in the right range of reps, for higher resistance and progressive overload, or for less resistance for warm-ups or endurance work, it will be wise to have **several sets of springs** at hand. One advantage of the jewel is that it is very easy to take apart to exchange the springs. When you build your own jewel, purchase only one set of four springs in the beginning, and test the tool with those when it's finished. If it feels to light or too heavy, don't despair. Keep the springs in any case, hit the hardware store again and purchase more sets of four lighter or tougher springs. It is also wise to have one set of four springs which give you a very hard time trying to squeeze the two boards together. Keep those as your "challenge springs", just like your challenge gripper. Keep training your thumbs and work towards those tough springs. You can even make your own little challenge of the jewel by always aiming to "close" all four springs, that is, pushing them together until the gaps between the spirals are fully closed (so they cannot be pushed together any further). This will give you a benchmark to measure your progress accurately. Let's say you "closed" the jewel five times this week, count this as five reps, then try to close it six times next week, progressively making more reps as you would with any other exercise. Then, after some time, use the next set of tougher springs, or your "challenge springs" and try to close them for several reps.

6) Thumb work on a gripper

You can also use your grippers to work your thumb, if not as comfortably and effectively. Instead of using the regular grippers it is advised here to use the **IMTUG**™ grippers which were designed by IronMind® specifically for such purposes. They have smaller handles and less resistance and are comparably comfortable for thumb work.

However, if you want to save your money and train your thumbs with a regular gripper you already own, here is what your can try. (But be well advised that this will only be possible with a very light gripper, one you will usually use for a light warm-up.) Let's say you want to train your right thumb. Take the gripper into your left hand, upside down, but in such a manner that about an inch of the bottom part of each handle is left to stick out from the top of your fist. Squeeze it until it is closed about half-way. Then grab the two ends of the handles sticking out from your left fist between your right thumb and curled right index finger, but in such a manner that the handle of the gripper is in a right angle to your thumb, not in a line with it. You will find the most natural position automatically once your try it. Then squeeze the gripper with your right thumb and index finger, but without letting go with your left hand, in order to keep the gripper steady, and also for safety.

Fig. 5.4 Thumb work on a gripper

Like I said, you will probably be barely able to close even a light gripper in this manner, so you might want to try one of the other ways of training your thumb described above instead.

Summary

- Pinch grip training is the perfect supplement to your crushing grip training, as it targets your finger tips and thumbs in particular.
- You should train your pinch grip with objects of varying width to train both your "open" (wide objects) and "closed" (narrow objects) pinch grip.
- Various objects can be used for training and testing: wooden blocks as described in the equipment section, barbell plates, or "blobs".
- In addition to static pinch grip training, it is not a bad idea to train your thumb dynamically. This is best done with a thumb machine or with a home-made jewel, as developed by Tommy Heslep.

Hint:

A strong pinch grip is especially useful for rock climbers, Freerunners, and Traceurs.

6. THICK BAR TRAINING

Here we will cover what thick bar lifting is, some variations of it, and why it builds great all-round grip strength.

Thick bar lifting trains your **open hand crushing grip**. Like the most pinch grip feats, this is a **static kind of strength**. What differentiates it from closed-hand crushing grip exercises, like hand gripper training, is that the **thumb is considerably involved**. Other than in the pinch grip, though, it is a more natural kind of grip - you have a better leverage and will be able to lift heavier weights. In some lifts, strong wrists are also of assistance. Tommy also points out the advantage of anatomy in these kinds of feats: "Having a big hand really helps out. With small hands like mine you need to work harder." Thick bar exercises are great all-round grip strength training, targeting fingers and thumb equally. Thick bar training also has the advantage that it can be done in passing, for example by slipping your Fat Gripz™ onto a barbell while doing curls, or simply by using a plate-loadable Olympic style thick bar for your regular lifts.

You need to differentiate between two kinds of thick bar challenges: **rotating and non-rotating weights**. If the weights can **rotate** freely on a plate-loaded thick barbell or a simple iron pipe as I suggested for this kind of training in the equipment section, you will be able to lift slightly more weight than with a **non-rotating** weight like an Inch-type dumbbell, or with the Apollon's Wheels, the original barbell of the oldtime strongman Louis Uni (which inspired the modern Apollon's Axle™). Objects like the latter two are just large chunks of iron. If they have a certain weight, they will simply roll from your hand. They will defy being lifted, even if they aren't that heavy!

> **Hint:**
> **The "Inch dumbbell" was the challenge dumbbell of the famous oldtime strongman Thomas Inch, which he allowed anyone to try to lift. Nobody managed to do so while Thomas Inch lived. He himself could overhead press (or bent-press) it even into high age and did so as part of his stage shows. It is extremely difficult to deadlift, let alone clean, because of its thick handle of 2 3/8 inches (c. 6 cm).**

Still, any type of thick bar device is more difficult to lift than the same amount of weight on a standard dumbbell or barbell, and makes great grip strength training.

Basically, thick bar exercises are just regular weightlifting exercises, so there isn't that much need for an exercises section here. But I want to add a few words on effective thick bar training and some popular exercises and feats.

1) Deadlifting

Deadlifting a heavy object with a thick bar handle is the basic exercise to test and train maximum open hand grip strength. The most famous challenges here are, again, one-hand deadlifting the Inch dumbbell (or a similar type of dumbbell) and the Rolling Thunder® with a varying amount of weight, or two-hand deadlifting a plate-loaded thick bar.

Now, deadlifting an **Inch replica** at 172 lbs (c. 78 kg) with one hand is an incredible feat. Here's how Tommy trained for it:

As with any training, the idea is that you approach your goal **step by step**. Don't just try to lift it over and over again although you can't. You will just go on failing. Instead, do this: Get a really good grip on the dumbbell with the hand you want to train. Then hold on with your other hand as well and perform a deadlift while holding it with two hands. Then give only as much assistance with your second hand as required - holding onto it with three, two, or only one finger - to hold it steady for at least a few seconds. Tommy worked his way up in this manner until he could hold the Inch dumbbell steady with one hand and only one finger of the assisting hand. Once he had accomplished this, the next step was to lift it with two hands, squeeze one of the globes between his inner thighs (just slightly to hold it in place), and then let go with the assisting hand completely. It worked, and eventually he was able to deadlift it one-handedly without any assistance at all.

You have to realize that it sometimes works better to lift the dumbbell two-handedly first, and then let go with as many fingers of the assisting hand as possible, instead of trying to lift it in the desired manner from the floor right away. It is less discouraging if you do it the first way in the beginning.

This knowledge is also helpful for a different kind of training with an Inch-type dumbbell, which could be called "negatives": Lift the dumbbell with two hands, as described above. Then let go with the second hand and fight fiercely as the dumbbell forces its way out of your hand. Make sure to try this on a surface which cannot be easily damaged - or outdoors - first. Also, don't try this in your flat if you live on any floor higher than ground level. Know that having 172 lbs of massive iron drop on the floor causes a considerable thump.

Tommy is the owner of a genuine Inch replica, but he has also found an elegant and comparably cheap way to build his own Inch-type dumbbells. When he hadn't messed with his replica for a while and wanted to get back into training, he decided to home-make his own, slightly lighter Inch-type dumbbell out of concrete. (He aptly christened it "Stonebell".) You might want to do the same to approach the Inch dumbbell step by step. Here is one way to do it: (This is my own version which I constructed according to Tommy's model. It doesn't look as fancy as Tommy's and is also much lighter, but it might do the trick.)

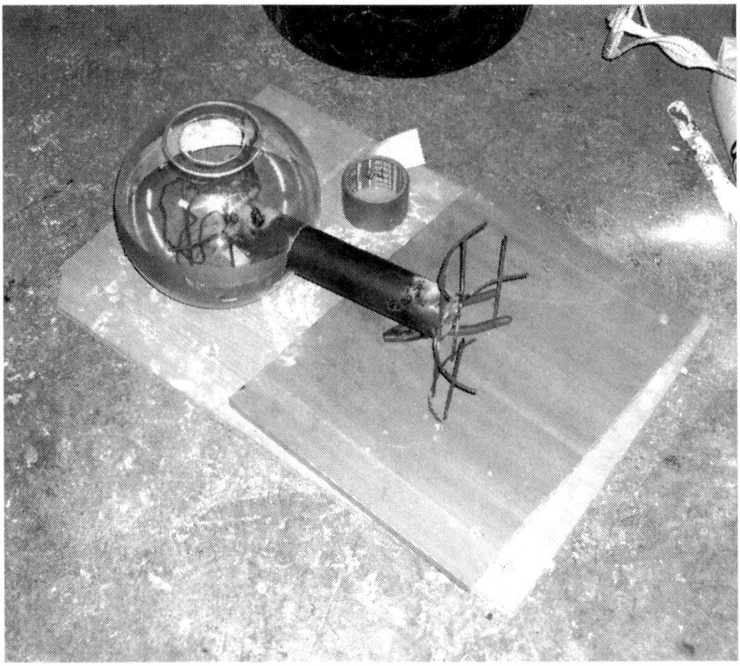

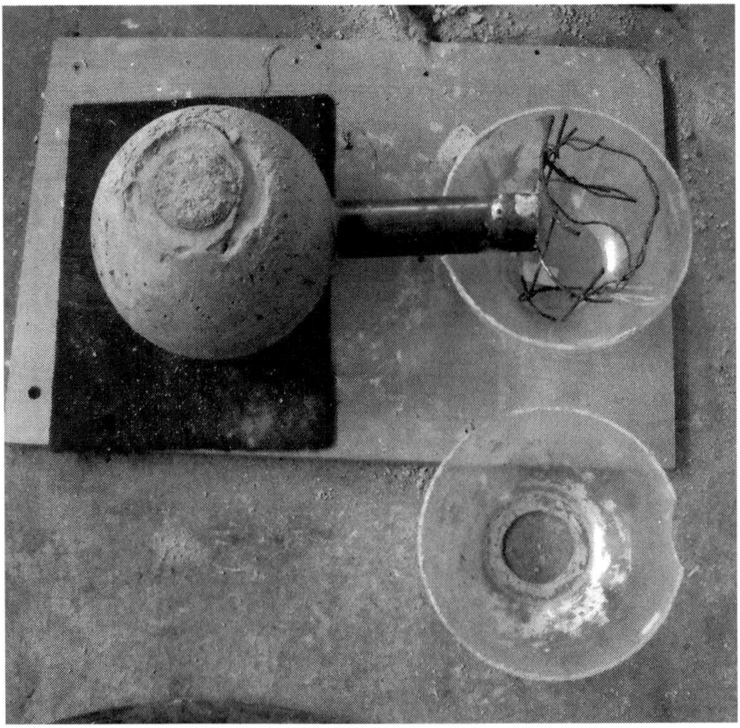

Grip Strength

Fig. 6.1 To cast your own "Stonebell", you need an iron pipe, two plastic bowls (half-spheric in shape), some wire, and concrete. Cut a hole into the bottom of one bowl, and two half-circle notches into the rim of each, so they leave a hole the diameter of the iron pipe when fitted together. Weld some wire to each end of the pipe to support the concrete and make the Stonebell more resistant against dropping. Fit the two plastic bowls over one end of the iron pipe after you have sprayed their inside with silicon spray and firmly close all holes (except the one on the top of the one bowl) with duct tape. Mix concrete and pour it into the sphere. Make sure to vibrate the concrete properly to get rid of excess air and water. Let dry for 12 to 24 hours. Cautiously remove the mould and repeat on other end of the pipe. If you get stuck, read instructions on how to pour your own Atlas Stone. Good luck!

Fig. 6.2 The finished Stonebell (left) with 90 lbs (c. 40 kg) and two other home-made Inch-type dumbbells weighing 132 lbs (c. 60 kg) (center) and 155 lbs (c. 70 kg) (right).

Deadlifting with a **Rolling Thunder®** is a whole other story. First of all, there is no bench mark in terms of a fixed weight that needs to be lifted, like the Inch's 172 lbs (although there are records to beat). You simply load it with weight plates, increasing the resistance in small steps when possible, and increasing your personal record. Thus, there is no need for the kind of "assistance with the second hand" method. (You can use it for severe negatives, however.) Secondly, and I already mentioned this, you will be able to lift slightly more overall pounds with a Rolling Thunder® than with an Inch-type dumbbell.[7]

Training with a Rolling Thunder® is pretty straightforward. To go for endurance, try to hold the weight for a longer amount of time. To increase your maximum strength, load the Rolling Thunder® with a weight you can hold for a few seconds at most, or which you can barely lift off the ground.

---

[7] Still, it won't be easy, because the handle of the Rolling Thunder - as the name says - rotates as well. The easiest way to lift weight with a thick bar handle would be a fixed handle attached on top of the weight - like a kettlebell with a thick bar handle. Then you could use a lot more wrist strength, because the handle wouldn't rotate.

Fig. 6.3 Deadlifts with a Rolling Thunder®. Note the self-made loading pin.

> **Hint:**
> Once you can deadlift 200 lbs (c. 90 kg) on a Rolling Thunder®, close a CoC® #2 gripper, and lift 45 lbs (c. 20 kg) with a pinch grip on the IronMind® Hub-Style Pinch Gripper, you qualify for IronMind®'s Crushed-to-Dust!® Challenge. See more at **www.ironmind.com**.

Then, of course, you can do regular deadlifts with a thick-handled barbell, with Fat Gripz™ on a regular barbell, or an Apollon's Axle™-type of device. Here, the aim shouldn't be to achieve your regular deadlift record, but to set your personal thick bar-deadlift record. If you really want to test your grip strength this way, I recommend you grab the barbell with a two-hand parallel overhand grip, similar to how an Olympic weightlifter would begin a clean or snatch, instead of the mixed grip the majority of powerlifters use and which helps them to keep a firm grip on the bar (with one palm facing outward and the palm of the other hand facing inward).

In any case, I recommend you learn the proper deadlifting technique before you try to set records in this manner. Get the help of a professional if you are unsure.

2) Cleans and Overhead Exercises

Deadlifting a heavy thick-handled object is a nice challenge and test of grip strength, but for some it is only half of the story. They want to see the weight being **cleaned and lifted overhead**. This can be done with an Inch-type dumbbell, or any type of thick-handled barbell, including a regular Olympic barbell with Fat Gripz™, or an Apollon's Axle™. While cleaning a thick bar object is indeed a feat involving considerable grip strength (but also technique and overall body strength), lifting it overhead requires only very little more grip strength than an object of the same weight with a regular handle would. Thus, when lifting if overhead, your shoulder strength and push press-technique will be the limiting factors, rather than your grip strength.

A few words on the Inch dumbbell in this context. You have learned about the original Inch dumbbell's dimensions: it weighs about 172 lbs (c. 78 kg), and its handle has a diameter of 2 3/8 inches (c. 6 cm). Now if you are into strongman competitions, you will say: "I have seen guys lifting a dumbbell of this kind, sometimes even a heavier one, and overhead lifting it for reps with one hand." That's true, but did you watch how they bring the dumbbell up to their shoulder? With two hands. However, the challenge is to do this with one hand only. What these Strongmen do are incredible feats of overhead strength, but the grip strength part, the actual reason why the dumbbell has such a thick handle, is almost completely ignored.

Well, there have been Strongmen who brought the Inch dumbbell to their shoulders and lifted it overhead with one hand only. One of them is Bill Kazmaier. But what he did was, he touched the dumbbell with other parts of his body at various stages of the lift. Perhaps he lifted it up to his hips, let it rest there for a second, brought it up to his chest, let it rest again, flipped it towards his shoulder, and push-pressed it.[8] An incredible feat from one of the strongest men who ever lived. Still, it isn't considered an official Inch dumbbell lift, because Bill didn't clean it properly and it touched other parts of his body apart from his hands. So to my knowledge **the only two people in the world who have officially lifted the Inch dumbbell with one hand overhead**, to the date I'm writing this, are Thomas Inch himself (who probably bent-pressed it instead of push-pressing it), and WWE wrestler Mark Henry (a well-documented event which caused a sensation in 2004), and some believe that Thomas Inch used a trick. One person who needs special mentioning is Laine Snook, who beautifully cleaned the Inch dumbbell at the Oscar Heidenstam (a British oldtime bodybuilding pioneer) Foundation dinner in 2008, demonstrating the same incredible grip strength and cleaning power

---

[8] That's how it could have happened, but I wouldn't know exactly.

as Mark Henry, but didn't lift it overhead, as he apparently lacked some of the mighty wrestler's shoulder strength.

So you will realize that in terms of grip strength, the best you can do is deadlift or clean an Inch-type dumbbell. The rest is shoulder strength and technique. As only three people in the world have managed to clean the Inch dumbbell "officially" at the moment I'm writing this, you are setting a high goal if you aim to achieve this. But there is always the Baby Inch at 117 lbs (c. 53 kg) or other Inch-type dumbbells at various weights to set your personal record.

To clean a thick-handled dumbbell with one hand, it helps to have trained regular **cleans with a barbell**, under the supervision of a professional Olympic weightlifter or a track-and-field athlete. It takes some time to learn the principle of firing up the barbell with full speed and power to dive underneath it just at the right moment (you don't have to squat down as low as Olympic weightlifters do, if you don't want to go for your absolute personal record). A clean isn't just a fast reverse barbell curl! Once you have mastered this movement, work your way up with a regular (narrow-handled) dumbbell. Usually you should soon be able to dumbbell-clean more than half of your regular barbell clean record with your stronger hand. Once you can handle the target weight of your thick bar dumbbell on a regular dumbbell easily - for example, 117 lbs (53 kg) if it's a Baby Inch replica - the only limiting factor will be your grip strength.

The same is true for cleaning a thick-handled barbell, which is a little less difficult, given the fact that cleaning a regular *bar*bell is easier to learn and execute than cleaning a regular *dumb*bell. I believe if you can clean a regular barbell properly, you can also clean a thick-handled barbell or a regular barbell with Fat Gripz™. The only limiting factor is your grip- and wrist-strength. So if you aim to set a new overhead press record with a thick bar, but fail on the clean, take some time to learn proper cleaning technique on a regular barbell first, with the help of a professional. (If you fail on the overhead press, this is not a matter of grip- but shoulder strength.)

What is considerably more difficult, however, is **cleaning proper Apollon's Wheels**. I'm sure you have seen these things, which look a bit like antique railway axles, in a strongman competition. Proper Apollon's Wheels have "plates" (they aren't actually plates, but rather resemble antique train wheels) on their ends which do not rotate on the bar but are firmly welded to it. This means you cannot rotate the bar without rotating the weights at its ends, making a clean much more difficult. If you have ever had a look at a new professional barbell as used in Olympic weightlifting competitions, from one of the leading companies who produce them, you will have realized how smoothly the ends rotate on their ball bearing. This helps the athletes to clean the barbell, because it is **less inert**. Apollon's Wheels, on the other hand, are more difficult to rotate in the air, and once they rotate, they are more difficult to be stopped from rotating, so they are much **more inert**. Thus, proper Apollon's Wheels behave differently from a regular barbell when being cleaned, and require learning a slightly different technique as well. Basically, you must try to clean it with as little rotation as possible, and take care to properly "dive" underneath it.

All of this is true if you consider cleaning Apollon's Wheels a feat of grip strength and dexterity. In the Strongman competitions you have probably seen, however, what counts more is the total weight being pressed overhead. Thus they have devised a way to slightly avoid the limitations of grip strength and technique. Many Strongmen grab the Apollon's Wheels with a mixed grip, like most powerlifters would when doing a proper deadlift. Then they perform a sort of very high deadlift, up to their belly or even their chest. Letting the bar rest on their huge thorax or stomach for a short moment, they change their grip, so that they hold it with an overhand grip. With a little bit of pushing and pulling, they bring the bar further up their chest, until they can perform a regular push-press.

If you are interested in hand strength primarily, however, try to clean Apollon's Wheels with a two-hand overhand grip from the start, and try keeping it from getting in contact with any other parts of your body but your hands.

3) Other Exercises

There are a number of other effective exercises you can perform with a thick-handled dumbbell or barbell, training your grip while working other muscles. I believe the most effective ones are the following: **rows, chins, biceps curls, reverse biceps curls**. In most of these exercises, using a thick bar or fatgripz will reduce the overall weight you can handle, limited by your grip strength. Still, it is a way to work on your upper-body and grip strength simultaneously.

Ultimately, you can do any exercise with a thick bar, even squats and bench presses. Brooks Kubik swears by using a thick bar for a great variety of exercises. Read his book *Dinosaur Training* to be inspired.

Summary

- Thick bar training is an effective and practical all-round way to improve your grip strength, as it involves your fingers as well as your thumb, and can be performed while doing exercises for the rest of your body, simply by performing regular exercises with thick bar equipment.
- Deadlifting a thick bar object is the basic challenge and can consist of a Rolling Thunder® lift, an Inch-type dumbbell lift, or a two-handed deadlift on a thick-handled barbell.
- A tougher challenge is to try to clean an Inch-type dumbbell or a thick-handled barbell. Learning proper cleaning technique first can be of great help here.
- Other effective exercises where you can train your grip in passing when using thick bar equipment are: rows, chins, biceps curls, and reverse biceps curls.

Hint:

Thick bar training is especially useful for grappling-based martial arts including wrestling and MMA, Freerunning and Parkour, and strongman competitions.

Robert Spindler with Tommy Heslep

7. ENDURANCE GRIP STRENGTH

As many sports require endurance grip strength rather than maximum grip strength, we want to suggest some ways of training for endurance.

In the last chapter you might have got the impression that I'm trying to slander the modern strongmen, saying their feats don't require grip strength. However, many of the most prominent modern strongman disciplines are actually brutal tests of grip strength - consider the Farmer's Walk or the Hercules Hold. Interestingly, however, those are tests of **grip strength endurance**, typically requiring to hold a certain weight for durations of around a minute or more. Usually, the competitor, who can hold onto the weight longest, wins. Other sports which are famed for requiring grip strength often require endurance grip strength rather than maximum grip strength as well, the best example being rock climbing.

Endurance and maximum strength in such sports go hand in hand. You need a certain amount of maximum grip strength to be able to even hold a 300 lbs (c. 135 kg) steel suitcase in one hand in the first place, before you can even consider walking around with it for a minute, doing a Farmer's Walk. The same goes for climbing. If you cannot hold your own bodyweight by your finger tips only, it's not much use if you can hold a tenth of it for half an hour. So even if your primary goal is to get better at a specific sport which stresses your endurance grip strength, you will also benefit from the maximum grip strength training we have concentrated on so far. But your focus will probably be some of the exercises below.

On the other hand, if your primary goal is maximum grip strength, you shouldn't neglect your endurance, and throw in one of the following exercises once in a while, remembering that a strong grip isn't complete if you cannot hang from a chin-up bar for longer than three seconds.

The most important thing about an endurance grip strength exercise is, in my point of view, that it gives you the possibility to **measure your progress** and **progressively and systematically increase your endurance** over time (just like a maximum grip strength exercise). The following exercises were chosen from the myriad of existing endurance grip strength exercises, because they give you the possibility to measure your progress fairly accurately and motivate you to push it to new heights. The idea is, basically opposite to a maximum strength exercise, to keep the weight resistance rather constant, and increase the duration of muscle tension. Try some of these popular ones:

1) Farmer's Walk

Everyone knows what the Farmer's Walk is, and it can be performed with different kinds of weights, from dumbbells to steel beams. It can be done for time, distance, or maximum weight. My gym colleagues and I often throw in a little challenge at the end of each workout session, and often this is a Farmer's Walk with 110 lbs (50 kg) dumbbells for laps around the gym. Being a rather easy weight, it definitely challenges your endurance, rather than your maximum strength. If you always use the same weight (it should at least be a *fairly* heavy weight), and try to increase the number of laps on a fixed circuit, you will push your grip strength endurance effectively and also condition your mind to "hang on".

2) Chin-ups on awkward objects or with limitations

If you are an athlete, you should be able to perform a certain number of chin-ups (not just one).

If not, lose some weight, or... do some chin-ups!

Doing chin-ups on odd objects and handles might limit the overall number of chin-ups you will be able to perform at first, but as your grip strength increases, your arm and back muscles will end up having a hard time to catch up. If you can do at least ten chin-ups on any of the following odd-objects of with the following limitations, you can consider such an exercise an effective boost to your grip strength endurance: thick climbing ropes, towels, a thick bar, Fat Gripz™, on your fingertips only (on an edge or a climbing board), on slings of thin rope (this exercise also trains your pain tolerance!), on three fingers per hand only, on two fingers per hand only, on one finger per hand only.

Fig. 7.1 Chin-ups on slings of thin rope are a great exercise to boost your grip endurance

Measure progress by increasing your reps.

At one point you should be able to do as many bodyweight chin-ups with the method of your choice as on a regular chin-up bar (meaning the strength of your arms and back becomes the limiting factor, not your grip). Following from there, you should try to increase the overall number of bodyweight chin-ups you are able to perform.

The advantage of this and the following exercise is that your weight resistance is your bodyweight, so (if it doesn't fluctuate too greatly) you always have a constant weight resistance, and your reps are the only thing you have to measure.

3) Hangs

If you have the feeling that chin-ups in the manner described above have a limited capability to push your grip strength endurance because your arm and back muscles always give in first, try this more straightforward exercise of simply **hanging from a chin-up bar** - or in any of the ways described above (climbing ropes, towels, etc.) - for time. Have a good, but merciless friend time your hangs with a stop-watch to avoid cheating on yourself. Gradually try to increase the amount of time you are able to hold on to a regular chin-up bar, ropes, towels, or and edge with your fingertips only. Especially here I would strongly advise you to keep track of your time and note it down for the next workout. Otherwise you won't be able to push yourself to a new personal record. Times of around a minute are a good benchmark, but there is really no limit.

A special variation of this exercise may be introduced here. It shall be called "Jouko Ahola Hangs", as the famous Finnish strongman Jouko Ahola is probably the one who made it popular. It is nothing else but timed hangs, but from a **revolving bar** - for example from a barbell laid on top of a power rack and not fastened in any way. If you try this for the first time, you will realize that it is much tougher to hold onto a revolving instead of a fixed bar. Doing this with a thick bar is a great way to prepare yourself for the kind of strength needed to lift Inch-type dumbbells, which tend to roll out of your hands much the same way the bar does here. Of course, you can also do chin-ups Jouko Ahola-style.

Fig. 7.2 Chin-ups on a thick bar Jouko Ahola-style. Note the thick bar (actually an aluminium pipe functioning as a thick bar) resting on the rack.

4) High-rep gripper training

Contrary to what we taught you earlier in this book, you may of course use a gripper for high-rep sets and thus train for endurance. Still, we would recommend you to use a heavy duty gripper instead of the cheap ones you find in your uncle's basement gym whose best days are long gone. Doing twenty-five CCS reps on a #1 CoC® Gripper is, in my opinion, much more effective than doing 250 reps on a plastic-handled gripper "toy".

To train for strength endurance with a heavy duty spring gripper, I would recommend you always use the same fairly strong gripper and try to increase the number of reps as you move along. Fifteen reps should be about the minimum to train for endurance rather than maximum strength. If you are primarily into maximum strength and equipped your private grip strength gym according to this need, your warm-up gripper might be the right one to train for endurance. Every once in a while, see how much reps you can squeeze out of it.

5) Strap holds for time

When I talked about this terrific exercise above (using a hand gripper, a strap, and a weight plate), I recommended to use as thin a strap as possible, as hard a gripper as possible, and as heavy a weight as possible to really make this an effective exercise for maximum closed-hand crushing grip strength, and to assist you in closing heavy grippers. However, strap holds are just as effective to train your grip strength endurance if you use **a lighter gripper, a lighter weight, or a thicker strap,** and squeeze the strap with the weight for time (10 seconds and upwards). The great thing about strap holds for endurance is the clarity: once the weight drops to the ground, you failed (take care not to squeeze the strap anywhere between gripper handle and the skin of your hand, as this is cheating). While your hand might open gradually in other exercises, giving you a few more seconds to "hang on", it's either "hold or drop" with strap holds. The dynamic is very different to other endurance grip strength exercises and you should definitely give it a try.

Ultimately, you can do almost **any grip strength exercise for endurance,** from pinching barbell plates to the Rolling Thunder. Find your favourites and perform them regularly.

Summary

- Many sports require endurance grip strength rather than maximum grip strength. At any rate, even if your primary goal is maximum grip strength, you should also train for endurance grip strength every once in a while, as a strong grip is not complete if it lacks the one or the other.
- Ideally, endurance exercises have only one variable which changes as your training progresses, to help you measure your progress accurately. Most often, this will be duration, sometimes reps.
- Some highly-effective endurance grip strength exercises have been recommended: the Farmer's Walk, chin-ups on odd objects or handles, hangs (including Jouko Ahola Hangs), high-rep gripper training, and strap holds for time.

> **Hint:**
> **Endurance grip strength is especially useful for rock climbers and strongmen.**

8. ADDITIONAL TRAINING
Here you will learn what other areas and muscles you should train to maximize your results and maintain healthy hands.

Basically, my recommendation would be to train your whole body - every major muscle group - and every aspect of physical fitness, including maximum strength, power, balance, stamina, etc. to become an all-round athlete and live a healthy lifestyle. But as the focus of this book is grip strength, I will limit myself to the aspects most clearly connected to hand strength. After all, the case may be that you have become intrigued by grip strength training because an injury forbid you to continue a sport you played before. Tommy, for example, had shoulder surgery and afterwards was unable to lift heavy, or do heavy shoulder or bench presses. So he focused on his grip and bending feats (which also provided a formidable upper-body workout) for four years. Only later would he incorporate kettlebell exercises and other stuff back into his routine.

If you can, work **all the muscles in your body** in one way or another. Either with barbells and dumbbells, or with kettlebells, bodyweight exercises, strongman equipment, or any other way you can think of.

But even if you are unable to train anything but your hands, for whatever reason, there is one muscle group you must train regularly at any rate: **your hand extensors.**

1) Hand extensors
If you could train only one other muscle group besides the muscles that close your hand, it would have to be this: the muscles that **open your hand**. Why? These small muscles on the upper side of your forearms seem of little concern, but they can cause a lot of trouble if ignored. If you train your grip intensely but disregard your extensors, the muscle imbalance can lead to cramps, shortenings, and eventually inflammations in your forearms, wrists, or elbows - all accompanied by pain and discomfort. Once you have a serious inflammation of your tendons, it will not only be hard to get rid of, but, needless to say, your progress will go down the drain.

Luckily, it is a rather widely known fact these days that hand extensor training is imperative to maintain hand health (although still too many individuals ignore it). In Tommy's days this knowledge was less spread. When he was training to close the #4 Captains of Crush® Gripper, he cut off all other training except gripper training for a year, and ignored a creeping pain in his middle finger tendon. Once he got certification for the #4 he immediately had to stop all grip strength training for the following year because the pain had become close to being unbearable. The tendon in his middle finger was really messed up.

Now Tommy acknowledges the usefulness of a balanced training routine. And although he managed to get certified for the #4 without any hand extensor training, he regrets not having learned about it earlier. It might have saved him a lot of trouble, pain, and discomfort: "I never thought opening the hand would help closing the gripper. I just didn't see that at the time. But I do now," he says.

There are few ways to train your hand extensors. An old-fashioned one would be to stick your closed hand into a **bucket filled with rice** or sand, then try opening it. This works quite well. If you take rice, for example, fill about 4 kg or 10 lbs of any kind of rice into a bucket, then stick your hand into it and try closing and opening it against the resistance. Feels great, doesn't it? You should be able to do at least 10 reps in a row without much effort.

Grip Strength

Fig. 8.1 The old-fashioned way of working your hand extensors: the bucket-of-rice-method

A more common method today is with **rubber bands**: Extend the fingers of your hand so they point away from you, then lift your thumb up as in a pinching movement, or as if you would want to imitate a duck's beak with your hand. Then wrap a rubber band around finger tips and thumb tip. The challenge is then to open your hand against the resistance of the rubber band.

It is a matter of debate how many reps and sets you should perform to train your hand extensors. Some do high-volume sets, aiming for numerous and fast reps. Others aim for high resistance and low reps, as with any other kind of strength training. A friend of mine, a rock climber and sports scientist, recommended doing sets of no more than 2-3 reps, but holding the extended position of each rep for about ten seconds when working with rubber bands. The logic behind it is that the hand extensors are muscles designed for stabilization rather than heavy reps. Try what suits you best.

Two to five sets, once or twice a week, should suffice. You can treat this training as part of a recovery session, incorporate it into your grip strength training (before, after, or in between your grip strength sets), or perform it on a separate day.

> **Hint:**
> **Doing push-ups on your closed fists also works your hand extensors.**

2) Wrists/forearms

The second thing you should train in addition to your grip and hand extensors are **the muscles that mobilize your wrists** (which are located in your forearms, just like most of the grip strength muscles). And there are a lot of them.

Why should you train your wrists? First of all, they will assist you in a lot of grip-strength feats, like thick bar lifting or tearing decks of cards. Secondly, I believe a strong grip is simply not complete without strong wrists. How intensely you will train your wrists is up to you, but you should do something at least.

To categorize the many muscles which mobilize your wrists, I suggest the following differentiation of muscle group pairs which move your wrists in complementary directions:

The **first muscle group pair** is the one which bodybuilders traditionally train with **wrist curls and reverse wrist curls**. If you make a fist and point your hand away from you as you would when performing a straight punch, back of the hand upwards, these muscles "curl" your hands upwards (as in a reverse wrist curl) and downwards (as in a wrist curl).

The **second muscle group pair** is the one used when **bending nails or levering a sledge-hammer**. If you make a fist again and hold it with your thumb upwards, as if holding a hammer to drive a nail into the wall, these muscles tilt your hand up and down on a vertical level. Actually, as if you were trying to hammer a nail into the wall without moving the rest of your arm. The muscles used to tilt your hand downwards are especially taxed in nail bending feats using the "underhand method" and those that tilt your hand upwards are taxed when the "overhand method" is used.

Keep your fist in the position just described, with thumb upwards. Now rotate it into the position described in the paragraph before that, where I explained the first muscle group pair. And back again. We consider the muscles, which make this movement possible, the **third muscle group pair**. Part of the work to perform this movement is done by your biceps. See your biceps moving as you **turn your hand clockwise and anti-clockwise**, as if turning a key in a lock?

The muscles which mobilize your wrists can be categorized in this way for training purposes. But the truth is, in everyday life and for many feats of strength you will often employ more than one group at the same time. That's why you should neglect neither of them.

The most popular ways to train the first group are **wrist curls and reverse wrist curls**, as mentioned. You can perform these with a barbell, with your forearms resting on a bench, or on your thighs when sitting, or simply with the bar behind your back or to your front while standing. Some find a SZ-bar especially comfortable for some of these variations - others dumbbells. Equally popular and easy to perform are **wrist-rolling exercises**. For these, you simply find a short wooden stick or iron pipe (you may use the same iron pipe as you use for thick bar training and barbell plate pinching) with a short piece of rope firmly attached to it. Attach a weight to the rope, then wind it up, using the strength of your wrists only, if possible. If you use an iron pipe, you can also slip it onto a stick or a narrow barbell which rests on a squat rack, so it doesn't move except rotating forward and backward. You will realize that you can wind up the weight in two ways, either by twisting the stick or pipe towards you or away from you. By alternating you can train both of the opposing muscle groups.

There are hundreds of other ways to train these muscles. Try them out for variation however you like.

Levering exercises are the most straightforward way to train the second muscle group pair. If you have a sledge hammer in your personal grip strength gym, as recommended in the equipment section, it will come in handy now. To train the muscles which tilt your hand up and towards you, when you hold it in front of you with your thumb pointing upwards, hold the hammer in your hand as if you would want to hammer a nail into the wall. Lower it as far as possible bit by bit, but so that you will still be able to lever it back up into the starting position. This is one rep. Aim for 6 to 8 reps. You can perform this exercise with your whole arm extended in front of you (more difficult), or your elbow by your side and only your forearm extended (easier).

Fig. 8.2 Levering exercises with a sledge hammer

    The opposing movement is performed in the following way: grab the hammer and hold it as if you would want to carry it on your shoulder, with your upper- and forearm at about right angles and the head of the hammer behind *your* head and pointing away from your back. But don't let the handle rest on your shoulder - instead, move it away from your shoulder so that you hold it only with your hand and it points toward the floor in an angle. Now try to lever it up until the hammer head points towards the sky behind your back - this is one rep. Alternately, extend your arm in front of you and hold the hammer so that it points right up towards the sky. Then lower the hammer head towards your face... and take care that in doesn't come crashing down! Practice in front of a mirror first, until you can manage this unusual movement. Observe the movement of your wrist - see how this is the opposite movement of the first levering exercise?

For both exercises, to increase or decrease resistance, grab the hammer farther down the handle, away from the head (more resistance), or farther up the handle, closer to the head (less resistance). If you do not have a sledge hammer among your utensils, practically the same exercise can be performed with an empty weightlifting bar. However, an Olympic bar will be too heavy for most. Try it with a 20 lbs (c. 10 kg) bar first. Grab it slightly off-center to increase the resistance, then lever it as you would a hammer to perform the exercises above.

The third muscle group pair, the complex muscles which rotate your wrist, or, to use the jargon, **pronate** and **supinate** it, are trained along the way if you do lots of different upper arm exercises. Dumbbell curls for your biceps, for example, train the muscles which supinate your wrist, and triceps extensions on a pulley, for example, train the muscles which pronate your wrist, if you use a rope as a handle and deliberately make the ends of it point outwards at the end of each rep. If you think this secondary stress isn't sufficient for these muscles, here is the easiest exercise to target them: again, grab a hammer or a light weightlifting bar and hold it in front of you as in the exercises described above. Now simply lever it, but neither to the front nor to the back, but to the left and the right, pronating and supinating your wrist while doing so.

Training all of these muscles will support your grip strength training and maintain your hand health. Naturally, you will get stronger wrists and forearms, and they might also increase in size. However, **don't confuse the size of your forearms with strength**. It is an old believe that big forearms equal a strong rip, but this is only true to a limited extent. Tommy found out early on that looks are deceiving when it comes to strength, and nothing is truer than that. Tommy, who is an avid nail and steel bender besides being a world-class grip strength expert, says his forearms and wrists increased only a little in size from all his wrist training, but he also points out that some guys have huge forearms but can't do nothing with the grippers or with nails. So don't spend too much time and worries on looks.

3) Hand muscles
We have been talking about all the muscles which **move your hands** now for a while, but the truth is, most of these muscles are located in your forearms. What about the muscles **located in your hands**? Apart from the thumb muscles, which will get apt training through pinch grip training and thick bar exercises, there are lots of small muscles in your hand which move your fingers sideways. The kind of muscles Mr. Spock uses to make his Vulcan

greeting gesture. How can these muscles be trained to maintain muscle balance and hand health? The most popular exercise for this is **finger walking**, and I believe the credit for it goes to John Brookfield once again. It is another exercise where your sledge hammer comes into play. This is how it is performed: Stand upright and hold the sledge hammer in your hand with the handle vertical and the hammer head close to the floor. Your hand should be in a position where your thumb is closer to the floor than the fingers. Basically, as if you had used it to hammer a nail into the wall and then lowered it. Now, try to "walk" your finger down the handle, that is, try to make the hammer head move towards your hand with your finger and thumb muscles only. In the beginning, this is quite tricky. But you will get the gist soon.

Grip Strength

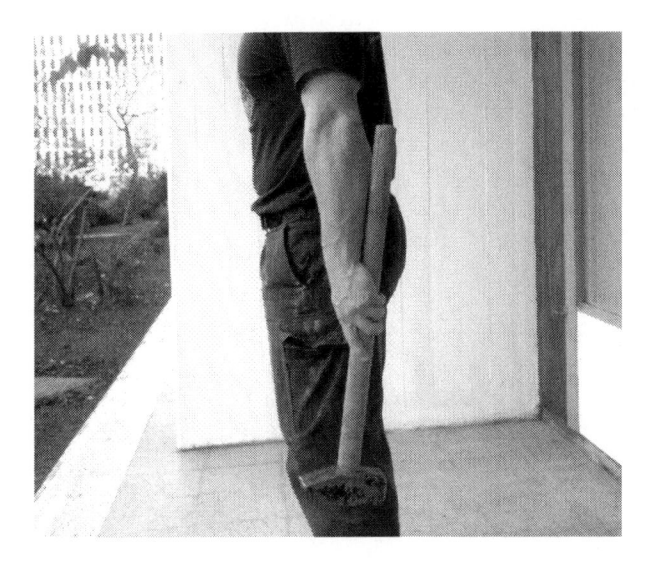

Fig. 8.3 Finger walking in one direction...

Fig. 8.4 ...and in the other. Always aim to bring the hammer head up until it touches your hand

For the opposite movement, which is even trickier, stand upright and hold the hammer in the same manner, but now with your thumb away from the floor. For this variation, you will need a considerable amount of thumb strength, but it will also train the little muscles in your hand which mobilize your fingers sideways.

If you don't have a sledge hammer, you can also perform these exercise with piece of wood, about the length of a sledge hammer handle and a 2 inch x 4 inch (5 cm x 10 cm) diameter. Tommy used both and says they are crucial exercise to assist you in closing big grippers.

4) Toughening and conditioning your hands:

If I were to test two men from an audience for their grip- or wrist strength with a mediocre feat they have never tried before, like closing a lighter gripper, crushing and apple, or bending a nail, and one of them was a young hobby bodybuilder with huge arms and the other a wiry, middle-aged craftsman, I would always bet on the craftsman first to achieve it. Why? Through years of hard manual labour, the hands of most craftsmen are conditioned in a way that they not only have a higher pain tolerance, but also that they develop a considerable maximum strength in their hands although they never trained for it. The principle behind this has been developed into a quite unusual training regimen by the nonconformist Pavel Tsatsouline, called "Grease the Groove". If you want to know more about it, read his book *The Naked Warrior*. Basically, it says that you can **gain maximum strength** in a specific movement not only by a conventional strength training routine, but also by **continual repetition of the movement with only mediocre resistance**, but over long periods of time. To make a long story short, conditioning your hands in everyday life with mediocre tasks can help you to build stronger and tougher hands in the long run. Don't shy away from carrying shopping bags and furniture, or fixing things around the house with your own hands. Just try new ways to tax your hands from time to time.

Of course, as you are following a tough grip strength routine, you must take care not to overdo it. Or, if you are a craftsman, it will probably not be necessary to tax your hands additionally.

5) Sports-specific grip strength training for gi-based martial arts

The grip strength training described in this book, if done correctly, will equip you with strong hands prepared for almost any situation in everyday life, any sport, and any feat of grip strength. However, I would like to introduce a sports-specific grip strength exercise here, because I found out it is very hard to do even if you have a fairly strong grip. This may be because it is more of a toughening exercise. Elite athletes in gi-based martial arts, like Judo or Brazilian Jiu-Jiutsu, can gain an advantage over their opponent if they are able to hold onto the tough fabric of a gi (the traditional Japanese clothing worn in such sports) with great power.

To train for this ability, they perform hangs or pull-ups from the specially designed training tool available for these exercises (as the "grip trainers" used in the illustrations below, from the company Scramble), or they use an old gi to make such a training tool on their own. Basically, all that is necessary are two gi-sleeves fixed to a chin-up bar - but they need to be sturdy enough and fixed in such a way that they can hold your bodyweight!

The illustrations below demonstrate three different ways to hold onto and to train with such a device. If you are a competitive martial artist, this kind of training only makes sense if you train the kind of grip which is allowed in your specific sport. In the illustration below, the way I hold onto the sleeves on the left picture is the easiest in my point of view. If you have a strong crushing grip you should be able to perform at least a few chin-ups in this manner. The way I hold onto the sleeves in the center picture is the hardest. For a start, it should suffice to perform hangs in this position for short periods of time. This is a very effective toughening exercise for your fingertips, so be prepared for some pain. The position in the picture on the right is somewhere in between.

Fig. 8.5 Pull-ups on gi-sleeves for gi-based martial arts (Judo, Brazilian Jiu-Jitsu, etc.)

Summary
- To lead a healthy lifestyle in general, to maintain hand health in particular and to maximize your grip strength potential, you should not only train your grip, but as many aspects of physical fitness as possible.
- If you have the possibility, train all muscle groups in your body with tools of your choice, be it dumbbells and barbells, machines, bodyweight exercises, kettlebells, strongman equipment, or the like.
- To avoid injuries through muscle imbalance, it is a high priority that you not only train those muscles which close your hand, but also those which open your hand. To do this, extend your hands in a bucket of rice or sand, or train with rubber bands wrapped around the four fingers and thumb of your hand, then work against the resistance by trying to open your hand.
- To achieve excellence in grip strength, it is wise to train the muscles which mobilize your wrists also. I differentiated between three muscle group pairs. To train all of them, do wrist curling and reverse wrists curling exercises, levering exercises in both directions with a sledge hammer or a weightlifting bar, and rotating exercises where you pronate and supinate your wrists.
- The little muscles in your hand which move your fingers sideways can best be trained by finger walking with a sledge hammer.
- Don't shy away from everyday tasks which tax your hands, in order to get stronger and tougher hands as a side effect.
- If you want to gain an advantage over your opponent in a gi-based martial arts, you can try to train and toughen your grip by doing pull-ups or hangs on gi-sleeves or with specially designed grip trainers for this purpose.

9. SAMPLE TRAINING ROUTINES

Here are some examples of how you could schedule your workout to cover all aspects of hand strength.

Now that you have learned about all kinds of grip strength equipment, exercises, rep-and-set schemes, the different types of grip strength, and additional areas you should train, we want to give you some idea of how you could structure your workouts. By now you will have realized that the number of grip strength exercises is endless and might ask yourself: how can I combine all of this in a simple training plan which leaves time for all my other activities during the week? Of course, the possibilities are endless as well, but I hope the following sample routines will help you to get some idea of what you routine *could* look like. In the end, however, you will have to put your own personal plan together, one which will take your spare time, ability to recover, and primary workout goals into account. In order to be able to do so, you have to be flexible, and willing to experiment and vary. Also, no training plan will be perfect forever. In order to make progress, you have to undertake changes every once in a while.

Example A) - "Grip & Wrist Strength Expert"

Note: This routine focuses on grip- and wrist strength, and is based on one of Tommy's schedules and adjusted according to his recommendations. Note that you train crushing and pinch grip, as well as wrists, twice a week each. The grip-specific workouts shouldn't take longer than an hour. As in all following sample training routines, Sundays are off and numbers of sets count for each hand.

Monday	Tuesday	Wednesday	Thursday	Friday
<u>Crushing grip:</u> 3 Warm-up sets of 10 with warm-up grippers Followed by: 3-4 closing attempts with challenge gripper Followed by: 5 negative sets with challenge gripper (singles, forced close with help of other hand)	<u>Wrist strength:</u> Variable wrist strength workout including exercises like wrist curls, reverse wrist curls, wrist-rolling, hammer levering, pronating and supinating hammer levering, or nail bending	Rest day with the following recovery session (repeated on Saturday): 2 sets of 20 of rubber ball squeezes Followed by: 2 sets of rubber band extensions (2 reps, hold for ten seconds) Followed by: 2 sets of finger walking with sledge hammer in both directions Followed by: 10 minutes of contrast baths Followed by: Light stretching of wrists and fingers in all directions	<u>Crushing grip:</u> 3 Warm-up sets of 10 with warm-up grippers Followed by: 5 negative sets (singles) with plate loaded grip machine, beyond the range Followed by: 3-4 strap holds with working gripper (no longer than ten seconds)	<u>Wrist strength:</u> See Tuesday
<u>Pinch grip training:</u> 3-4 sets of static holds with weighted 2x4 wooden block (no longer than ten seconds), progressively increasing the weight each set			<u>Pinch grip training:</u> 3-4 pinch grip record attempts with plate-loaded iron pipe Followed by: 5 sets of dynamic thumb	

Grip Strength

Followed by: 3-4 sets of static holds with weighted 4x4 wooden block (no longer than ten seconds), progressively increasing the weight each set			training on thumb machine or "jewel"	

Example B) - "Athlete"

Note: This is a routine for someone who wants to complement his regular weight training with grip-specific training. Hence it is a little more time-saving. The grip-specific workouts shouldn't take longer than half an hour. It is also suitable for someone who needs more recovery time, as it focuses on each kind of grip- and wrist strength only once a week. It splits the wrist muscle group pairs into two and pairs them with finger extensor training on Monday and thick bar training on Friday. Wednesday should be an economic and intense crushing grip training.

Monday	Tuesday	Wednesday	Thursday	Friday
Regular weight training for upper or lower body followed by:		Regular weight training for upper or lower body followed by:	Rest day with the following recovery session (repeated on Saturday):	Regular weight training for upper or lower body followed by:
3-4 sets of 6-15 of reverse wrist curls in variations		3 Warm-up sets of 10 with warm-up grippers	2 sets of 20 of rubber ball squeezes	3-4 sets of 6-15 of wrist curls in variations
Followed by:		Followed by:	Followed by:	Followed by:
3-4 mediocre overhand nail bends		1-3 sets of 2-10 with working gripper	2 sets of finger walking with sledge hammer in both directions	3-4 mediocre underhand nail bends
Followed by:		Followed by:		Followed by:
3-4 sets of rubber band extensions (3 reps, hold for 10 seconds)		3-4 negative sets with challenge gripper (singles, forced close with help of other hand)	Followed by: 10 minutes of contrast baths Followed by: Light stretching of wrists and fingers in all directions	3-4 sets of static holds with thick bar dumbbell (no longer than ten seconds), progressively increasing the weight each set
		or		
		3-4 negative sets (singles) with plate loaded grip machine, beyond the		

		range		
		or		
		3-4 strap holds with working gripper (no longer than ten seconds)		

Example C) - "Grip Strength Expert"
Note: This routine really focuses on the different kinds of grip strength and only does the necessary minimum for wrists. It trains the specific grip-strength kinds only once per week, but then it does so with brutal intensity.

Monday	Tuesday	Wednesday	Thursday	Friday
Crushing grip:	Rest day with the following recovery session (repeated on Thursday and Saturday):	Pinch grip:	See Tuesday	Thick bar:
3 Warm-up sets of 10 with warm-up grippers		Warm-up with light holds on 2x4 and 4x4 wooden blocks		Warm-up deadlifts with empty thick-handled barbell
Followed by:		Followed by:		Followed by:
1 set of 2-10 with working gripper	2 sets of 20 of rubber ball squeezes	1 pinch grip record attempt with plate-loaded iron pipe		1 record attempt with thick bar dumbbell
Followed by:	Followed by:			
1 record attempt with challenge gripper	2 sets of light hammer levering in both directions	Followed by:		Followed by:
		3-4 sets of static holds with weighted 2x4 wooden block (no longer than ten seconds), progressively increasing the weight each set		5 sets of 6 of deadlifts with thick-handled barbell, progressively increasing the weight each set
Followed by:	Followed by:			
5 negative sets with challenge gripper (singles, forced close with help of other hand)	2 sets of finger walking with sledge hammer in both directions			Followed by:
				5 sets of static holds with thick bar dumbbell (no longer than ten seconds), progressively increasing the weight each set
Followed by:	Followed by:	Followed by:		
5 negative sets (singles) with plate loaded grip machine, beyond the range	10 minutes of contrast baths	3-4 sets of static holds with weighted 4x4 wooden block (no longer than ten seconds), progressively increasing the weight each set		
	Followed by:			Followed by:
	Light stretching of wrists and fingers in all directions			2 sets of heavy wrist-rolling with thick wrist
Followed by:				
1 strap hold				

with working gripper (no longer than ten seconds) until total failure Followed by: 1 set of 2-10 of reps with gripper upside down with warm-up gripper Followed by: 2 sets of rubber band extensions (2 reps, hold for ten seconds)		Followed by: 3-4 sets of dynamic thumb training on thumb machine or "jewel" Followed by: 2 sets of rubber band extensions (2 reps, hold for ten seconds)		roller in both directions Followed by: 2 sets of rubber band extensions (2 reps, hold for ten seconds)

Example D) - "Simplicity & Endurance"

Note: This routine is for anyone who seeks simplicity and wants to build good all-round grip strength to support him in other endeavours, like his primary sport. It includes exercises for grip strength endurance and aims to reduce the additional training time for grip strength to a minimum, incorporating many exercises which train other body parts simultaneously with the grip.

Monday	Tuesday	Wednesday	Thursday	Friday
<u>Thick bar & endurance:</u> Regular weight training for upper or lower body (e.g. back training) including: Deadlifts with thick bar or Fatgripz on regular barbell Followed by: Chin-ups on climbing ropes, slings of thin rope, or on finger tips	Rest day with the following recovery session (repeated on Thursday): 2 sets of 10-15 of rubber ball squeezes Followed by: 2 sets of 10-15 of rubber band extensions (hold for 2 seconds)	<u>Wrist strength:</u> Regular weight training for upper or lower body (e.g. arm training) including: Triceps extensions on rope pulley Followed by: Hammer curls *or* Reverse barbell curls *or* Dumbbell curls Followed by: Barbell wrist curls	See Tuesday	<u>Crushing grip:</u> Regular weight training for upper or lower body followed by: 3 Warm-up sets of 10 with warm-up grippers Followed by: 1-3 sets of 2-10 with working gripper Followed by: Maximum reps with light warm-up gripper for endurance

Grip Strength

Example E) - "Old-School Volume Gripper Training"

Note: Not recommended for beginners. Give this routine a try if you are at an advanced level with the grippers and progress absolutely stagnates. The extreme volume will be a shock not only for your grip muscles, but also for your tendons and ligaments, so be cautious. The plan itself is a rather simple old-school routine - but don't be fooled, as the high number of sets and the repetitiveness demand great concentration and determination to carry each session through to the end. Start with 30 sets on the gripper/machine negatives and do 5 sets more each week until you reach 40 sets. then increase the weight on the machine and start again with 30 sets, working your way up in that manner, while you stick with 40 sets of gripper negatives or gradually increase the number to 50 or more sets. Make it your aim to make the last five sets of the gripper/machine negatives the hardest of the day. Measure progress on your challenge gripper every once in a while.

Monday	Tuesday	Wednesday	Thursday	Friday
<u>Crushing grip (gripper work)/pinch grip:</u> 30-50 negative sets with a gripper heavier than your challenge gripper (singles, forced close with help of other hand or on thigh) 10 minutes of hand extensions in bucket of rice or sand (alternating hands, 10-15 reps each time) 10 minutes of lifting blobs (alternating hands, holding blob as long as	Rest day with the following recovery session (repeated on Saturday): 2 sets of 20 of rubber ball squeezes Followed by: 2 sets of finger walking with sledge hammer in both directions Followed by: 10 minutes of contrast baths Followed by: Light stretching of wrists and fingers in all directions	<u>Wrist strength:</u> Wrist strength exercises as desired		<u>Crushing grip (machine work)/ pinch grip:</u> 30-40 negative sets (singles) with plate loaded grip machine, beyond the range 10 minutes of hand extensions in bucket of rice or sand (alternating hands, 10-15 reps each time) 10 minutes of lifting blobs (alternating hands, holding blob as long as possible each time) 1 set of

possible each time) 1 set of maximum reps with rubber ball (100+ reps) or light gripper (20+ reps)				maximum reps with rubber ball (100+ reps) or light gripper (20+ reps)

> **Hint:**
> **Using a timer or Gymboss® to time the breaks between your sets can help keep count of your sets and prevent your workout from taking longer than needed - especially when it's a high volume routine.**

Robert Spindler with Tommy Heslep

10. GRIP STRENGTH FEATS

In this chapter you will learn of some classic feats of grip strength and how to perform them.

Once you have achieved a level of considerable grip strength, you might want to test it with some classic feats of strength or demonstrate it to your friends in a fun and impressive way. As Tommy pointed out to me, the grippers are a good way to train and test your hand strength, but one only relatively few people can relate to. Only someone who has tried a certain gripper beforehand knows how difficult it really is to close, so if you demonstrate this in front of a larger audience where you cannot give everybody the opportunity to try, most of them will leave relatively unimpressed. The fun about the following grip strength feats, however, is that they are performed with **everyday objects**, so that almost anyone can immediately go home and try them on their own - and fail.

Myriads of grip strength feats of this kind exist, and the following is only a small choice of some popular ones. I have tried to include only such feats which stress grip strength first and foremost, although, typically, other muscles are involved as well. Feats which stress other muscles primarily and your grip only secondarily are not included.

Remember that such feats of strength are called feats of strength because **not everyone is expected to perform them**. So don't be disappointed if you cannot do some them even at an advanced training level - because this is actually a good thing! Let me explain: the more difficult the feat is, the more exclusive it is, and the less people can imitate it. So, if you have to invest several years of training to achieve them, this means there are less people who can do the same. And this is how it is supposed to be. (For those of you who cannot wait to have fun with their grip strength I included some lighter feats which someone at an intermediate level - but no beginner - should be able to perform.)

1) Crushing Potatoes and Other Food

When it comes to crushing food with the hand as a demonstration of grip strength, the potato is clearly the supreme discipline. But before I cover the potato, I want introduce you to two types of food which also make for formidable grip strength demonstrations, although they are a lot easier to destroy: walnuts and apples.

Were you ever faced with the situation that you were sitting in front of a bowl of **walnuts**, still in their shell, and felt in need for some healthy fatty acids, but there was no nutcracker in sight? Next time you are, try this: place two walnuts into your palm next to each other in the same manner you would place the handles of a CoC® Gripper into your palm. One of them needs to be right in the middle of your palm, resting against the thumb pad so it won't slip away. Then you put the other one right next to it, towards the fingers, so that the nuts touch. Now close your hand around them powerfully and imitate the movement of closing a gripper. If you are lucky and strong enough, the shell of one walnut will burst as the one with the tougher shell is pressed against it. As is the nature of any feat of strength involving organic material, this feat will be tougher to perform one time, and easier the next time, depending on the degree of hardness of each individual nut. Sometimes they will burst with only little pressure, the other time you will have to face defeat. But in general it is a fun way to test and demonstrate your grip strength - and practical too.

Most readers will know someone who can halve an apple with two hands - plenty of you will regularly do this themselves - but this is a feat where a lot of technique is involved. **Crushing an apple with only one hand**, however, is more of a pure grip strength feat, and a lot more fun (and a lot messier as well). When I asked Tommy whether he had also tried to crush other objects besides potatoes, for example an apple, he confirmed and added - "that apple was a joke!" While crushing an apple in one hand is no challenge to someone with a world-class grip like Tommy's, you will find that most John Does can't do it. As with nuts, of course, it always depends on the individual apple - its size, its quality, and its degree of ripeness. But let's assume you have an apple which is average in all of these parameters. Then it surely takes some grip strength to crush it with one hand, especially if you want to do it fast for a better effect. But it is doable. Now, there are two ways to do this - an easier one and a more difficult one. The easier and more common one is to drive your fingertips right into the apple and then finish it off with the same motion as you would close a gripper. Imagine using your four fingers like one large, blunt blade to cut the apple in half. Although you are actually halving the apple rather than "mashing" it, it will give a similar impression if you do it fast, because you will indeed mash the one half which remains in your hand as you finish the movement.

The more difficult way, and some would argue the more "genuine" way, is to wrap you fingers around the apple as if it was a baseball you are about to hurl, or as if you would pick up a thick bar. Then simply close your hand and hope that the apple will collapse. You will notice that this is considerably more difficult to do, with the same kind of apple, than the first method. With a larger apple, you will even find it an impossible feat.

Now let's talk about **potatoes**. This is an almost legendary feat and only few can do this (with an uncooked potato, of course). The athletic German actor Raimund Harmstorf demonstrated this feat - unfortunately with a cooked potato - in the TV-mini-series *Der Seewolf* (1971), an adaptation of a

Jack London adventure story. Audiences enjoyed this scene so much that Raimund was to be remembered for it for the rest of his life in the German-speaking world. Tommy Heslep is an expert at crushing potatoes, as he demonstrated in the *Tonight Show* with Jay Leno in 2007, where he crushed 12 potatoes in a row in quick succession - that is, within 15 seconds (!). When I asked him if there is any secret to this feat he answered in the negative and added that all this feat requires are **a strong crushing grip, great pain tolerance, and short fingernails**. The way to do it is the same as the first method to crush apples described above. You actually drive your fingernails into the potato and finish it off like closing a gripper (this is the only way to crush a raw potato with one hand - to crush one with the second method for crushing apples described above is impossible). Once you are able to do this with an average potato, you can count yourself to an elite of grip strength athletes and are probably on a level where you can at least close the #3 CoC® easily. Note that the larger the potato and the wider your hand is open, the harder it is going to be. To train towards it, you may want to start off with apples, using harder ones as you move along. Tommy couldn't do it the first time he tried, and the pain was one of the major problems. He would only try it once every other month until he could do it.

2) Tearing Decks of Cards

Tearing a whole deck of cards (52 cards, plus - perhaps - jokers), is a feat of strength that will seem impossible to most who try it the first time. However, a combination of **excellent grip strength, technique and practice** makes it possible. Tommy taught it himself. The technique he uses is the following: imagine the deck of cards standing upright in the air, with the narrow side towards you. One of your hands - let's say the left one - grabs the upper edge of it from the left, the other, your right hand, grabs the lower edge of the deck from the right. To tear the deck in half, twist your left hand in a counter-clockwise motion (if looking on it from above), and your right hand in a clockwise motion and imagine to move your hands apart at the same time. This is one technique, but it isn't the easiest one. However, it is one of the faster ones if you are strong enough.

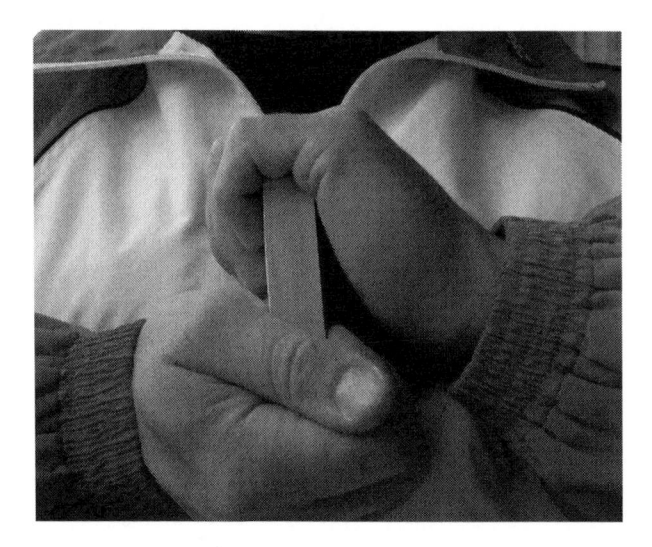

Fig. 10.1 One way of card tearing, preferred by Tommy Heslep

An easier, but slower technique would be to hold the deck in a similar way as above, but with the top of your left hand (that is, the fingers), on that edge of the deck which points away from you. Then you would start by twisting your hands in opposite directions as described above. The upper (left) hand clockwise, and the lower (right) hand counter-clockwise.[9]

---

[9] There are plenty of different techniques and variations to this feat, but they cannot all be covered here in detail. For anyone who wants to go deeper into it, Jedd Johnson has compiled a whole e-book on it - *The Card-Tearing E-Book*. Check it out.

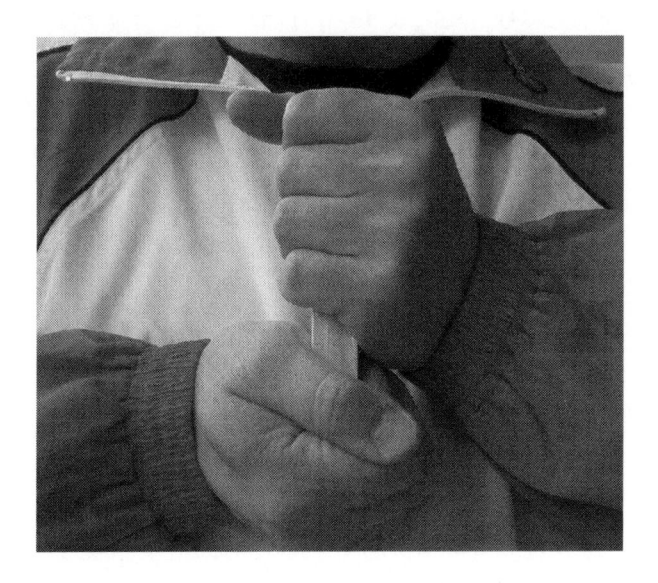

Fig. 10.2 Another way of card tearing

To learn the proper technique and become strong enough to do a whole deck of cards, buy a couple of cheap decks and **start practising with very few cards at first**, say ten or twenty, then work your way up to more. It is probably a good idea to start with this once you have already developed a solid basic grip. Else you will waste a lot of money on cards, training towards it regularly and not getting there fast enough. If you are lucky you will find a toy store which sells bare, white cards (to be designed by the buyer himself) - which are usually rather cheap - for practice. Working your way up by gradually increasing the number of cards you tear in half each time you try is a better way of achieving your goal than trying a full deck over and over again and leaving frustrated each time you fail.

If you want to save your money on the deck of cards a bit, you might want to try building your own "**jewel**", as described in the equipment section. Tommy used this home-made tool to practise the described technique for card-tearing he applies. As the hand position in this grip strength feat is completely different from all other feats and training methods described so far, Tommy tried to think of a way to train this kind of strength more specifically, and with reps. This is how he came up with the jewel.

Now, there *is* another way to train this grip strength feat, but I would recommend it only to athletes who already have a grip above average, some pain tolerance and a strong willpower. It is basically the method which Tommy used to tear his first deck of cards. What you do is, take a whole deck of cards and simply **begin to work at it**, trying different techniques and hand positions, for as long as you like, taking breaks when necessary. But **don't stop until you have torn the whole deck in two.** Be aware that your fingers might hurt for several days after. But believe me, it's a highly effective way to train exactly the kind of strength you need to tear decks of cards. In the beginning it might take you half an hour to tear it in half, but if you try it again and again every other week, you won't need more than half a minute eventually (I guess Tommy does it in less than half a second).

Note that although this feat requires wrist and upper-body strength as well, the weak link is still your grip. The challenge in this feat is basically to squeeze the deck hard enough to go through the whole of it, because else you will only rip off a few cards on the outside. Good luck!

3) Lifting the Dinnie Stones

Especially since the publication of Steve Jeck's *Of Stones and Strength*, the Dinnie Stones have gained worldwide recognition as an old-fashioned test of strength. The ultimate challenge, lifting the two stones without any assistance such as lifting straps, is a thorough test of overall body strength (similar to a deadlift), but the limiting factor are the ring-shaped handles on the two stones. This makes them a feat of grip strength after all.

Originally, the stones, still resting outside the Potarch Hotel near Crathie in Scotland, served a different purpose. But when the Scottish Highland Games champion and oldtime strongman Donald Dinnie lifted them bare-handed and carried them across the width of the nearby Potarch bridge in the late 19th century, they turned into a notorious and, for a long time, unconquered test of strength. In the course of the 20th century, every time someone managed to lift them (assisted first, then unassisted, starting with Jack Shanks in 1973), this caused a little sensation. In recent years, the number of men who try them has increased, and so has the number of successful lifters. In all fairness, it needs to be added that the stones have been weighed on different occasions, and they have actually lost some weight over the years, probably due to little chips and chunks splitting off from the many attempts to lift them. They used to weigh 775 lbs (c. 351 kg) altogether, now their combined weight is 734 lbs (c. 332 kg). Now, the smaller stone weighs 321 lbs (c. 146 kg), the larger one 411 lbs (c. 186 kg).

Still, I included the following picture not without a little pride. It documents my successful unassisted lift of the stones on 26 July 2013.

Fig. 10.3 Lifting the Dinnie Stones

As you can see in the picture all I used was a bit of chalk on the hands, but no lifting straps and not even a belt.

I trained for this feat in the following manner: I separated the training for the specific grip strength and the training for the top-position deadlift strength. The first thing I did was to ask my welder to make two Dinnie-Ring replicas for me. I did not know the exact measurements, but settled for two identical rings with an outer diameter of 7 1/4 inch (18 cm) and a thickness of 5/8 inch (16 mm). As it turned out, the original ring on the smaller stone was a little bit smaller, and the original ring on the larger stone was a little bit larger - which made it easier to lift than I thought.

Fig. 10.4 Ring replicas for Dinnie Stone training

    I then trained my grip for the feat in a very straightforward way: I simply worked my way up with alternating one-handed deadlifts with one replica ring and a loading pin. All I did was about five single sets per hand, with about three minutes rest in between, and increasing the weight on each attempt and each week. I reserved one day per week for this training only. Basically, what you recquire to lift the Dinnie Stones is a strong crushing grip - but training with grippers alone will not prepare you the ideal way for the odd pain the Dinnie Stones cause on the skin of your hand. To toughen my hands additionally, I would do 3-5 sets of as many chin-ups as I could on the replica rings on a separate day.

    Also on a separate day I would then train my specific top-position deadlift strength. I am naturally strong when it comes to top position deadlifts in a rack, but the fact that you have to lift the stones with one hand in front and one hand behind your body calls for specific attention. I thus tried to duplicate the situation as closely as I could:

Fig. 10.5 Dinnie Stone deadlift training with a barbell

I slid the two ring replicas onto a barbell which I loaded with weight unevenly - to simulate the feeling of having to lift two stones with a different weight. Then I would straddle the bar and work my way up with the odd deadlifts until I could do three reps with 728 lbs (330 kg) on the last training before my plane left for Scotland. I would usually do two to three warm-up sets and then three working sets, increasing the weight each time and reducing the numbers of reps, for example, 5-4-3. However, for the deadlift training I used lifting straps to go easy on my grip (which I trained hard on the separate day).

Having worked my way up with these devices, lifting the actual stones appeared surprisingly easy. Good luck!

4) Chinning on Rafters
This is a feat of strength for **pinch grip experts** with a very **light bodyweight**. To do a two-handed chin-up on two rafters, first of all you need... rafters! But if your house doesn't have them of you don't have access to a loft, it should be the least problem to build a simple device of two beams with the proper thickness and spacing to perform this feat. You could, for example, fix two 2 inch x 4 inch (c. 5 cm x 10 cm) wooden beams to the top of a power rack.

The greater problem will be to build such a tremendous pinch grip strength that you can hold half your bodyweight in one hand in the desired manner. If you weigh well above 200 lbs (c. 90 kg) you might want to find different goals to pursue than this feat. But let's say you weigh 160 lbs (c. 72 kg). Then it should be possible. But you must be able to pinch grip at least 80 lbs (c. 36 kg) in your weaker hand for the duration of one chin-up. At least! Because, simply supporting your bodyweight by pinching two rafters in one thing, but doing a chin-up is a whole other story. First of all, it takes time to do a chin-up, so you have to sustain the grip for several seconds. Secondly, your grip will not only be taxed in a vertical direction by the resistance of your bodyweight, but also from all sorts of other angles as your center of gravity shifts during the movement. This is also the reason why it is much easier to begin a chin-up on rafters with slightly bent elbows rather than with completely straight arms.

To work towards this feat, begin by training your pinch grip seriously, until you can pinch and lift about 60% of your body weight with your weaker hand, for example with weighted wooden blocks. Then begin step-by-step work on the rafters with specific exercises. You could do chin-ups where you hold a rafter only with one hand, but a regular bar with the other. Once you can maintain your bodyweight on the rafters, but can't do a chin-up, do timed hangs on the rafters. As you grow stronger and more familiar with this kind of challenge for your pinch grip, begin with negatives: Step onto a chair so that you are high enough to start from the end position of a chin up. Pinch the rafters, step off the chair, and try to fight gravity as you perform a forced "negative chin-up". As a next step you can try regular chin-ups on the rafters, starting with bent elbows. If you work hard, maybe one day you will be able to do a chin-up on rafters starting with straight arms!

Summary
- Don't be discouraged if you cannot achieve a certain grip strength feat the first time you try, even if you believe you have formidable grip strength already. Remember that the more difficult a feat of strength is, the more exclusive it is, and once you do achieve it, it will be all the more worth.
- To crack walnuts with your hand, place two of them closely together into your palm and then close your hand in the same motion as you would close a gripper. Most of the work will be done by your middle finger.
- To crush an apple with one hand the easier way, drive your fingers into it as if they were a blunt blade, practically halving it, then finish it off by crushing the half remaining in your hand as you would "crush" a gripper.
- To crush an apple with one hand the harder way, hold it like a baseball you are about to hurl and them attempt to close your hand, "crushing" the apple in the truer sense of the word.
- Crushing a raw potato with one hand is in fact a world-class grip strength feat. Perform it in the same way as the easier way to crush an apple - by driving your fingers into it as if they were a blade. This feat not only requires a strong crushing grip, but also great pain tolerance.
- There are several techniques to tear a deck of cards in half. Find yours and progressively increase the number of cards you tear in half in one go, starting with, perhaps, 10 or 20. To save money on cards, you might want to train the specific hand strength required for this feat with your own home-made jewel (see equipment section).
- To lift the Dinnie Stones, I found it helpful to get a hold of two Dinnie Ring replicas. I then trained on two separate days per week, training my grip with one-handed ring replica deadlifts on the first day, and my deadlift strength with two-handed, lifting strap-supported, deadlifts with the ring replicas on an unevenly loaded barbell on the second day.
- To practice chinning on rafters, build up great pinch grip strength first. Then work your way up with specific exercises such as pinching a rafter with only one hand, but holding onto a bar with the other hand, "negative chin-ups" on rafters, and then go on to regular chin-ups, but starting with bent elbows.

Robert Spindler with Tommy Heslep

11. RECOVERY, PLATEAUS, AND INJURY PREVENTION

Here you will learn what to do to overcome plateaus, how to optimize recovery between workouts and from injuries, and how to avoid injuries in the first place.

In the context of strength training and muscle building it cannot be explained often enough to the beginner that **your muscles grow**, not while you are training, but **while you are resting**. Therefore, recovery between workouts is essential. It's a simple chain of thoughts: The harder you train, the better your results will be, but the more you must rest to recover from your workouts. If you do not recover enough because you rest too little, your progress will stagnate and you will reach a plateau. Keep on training with the same intensity and you are likely to get injured. And I do not need to mention that any injury throws you back along your path at least a couple of weeks. And the less optimized your circumstances for recovery from this injury are, the tougher this setback will be. Suboptimal recovery, plateaus, injuries, and suboptimal recovery from these injuries - this vicious cycle is your biggest enemy in making progress with your grip strength.

11.1. Recovery

So we want to ensure proper recovery as much as we want to train with full intensity. The one without the other will keep us from reaching our full potential in the shortest time possible.

What if you could **speed up that process of recovery**? You would reach your goals much faster, and you would probably reach goals you wouldn't otherwise. Training would be a lot more fun. This is the reason why so many young men reach for muscle-enhancing drugs and make fast progress in becoming huge and strong. Because of the side effects and legal issues, however, the fun is going to stop sooner or later, so we strongly recommend to avoid this short cut. The good news for you is: 1) As Tommy (a natural grip strength athlete) demonstrated on his own body, you can gain "superhuman" grip strength without any steroids at all (this observation was confirmed to Tommy in many conversations with other grip strength experts, who generally acknowledged that steroids are of little use to grip strength gains). 2) There are natural methods to ensure an optimized recovery in between grip strength workouts.

Here are some of them (most of this has been foreshadowed in the Sample Training Routines section above):

1) Light training

Basically, the idea behind each strategy for muscle recovery is to **increase the blood circulation** in the specific muscle, so that more blood can transport the nutrients necessary for recuperation into the muscles faster and more effectively (this is a simplified version of complex biochemical processes). But you are also looking for ways to relax muscles which are tensed up from training. One simple and straightforward way to do both is to perform the same exercises or movements you would perform to *train* the muscles, but with very **light intensity**. It seems paradox to use the muscles again to actually help them recover, but this is how it works. The light training pumps blood into the muscles again, which assists in repairing them, but without causing all the little micro-injuries we usually inflict on purpose with an intense workout (and from which the muscles need to recover). And flexing muscles without maximum intensity and releasing them fast can diminish the tension in the muscles which has built up in the course of heavy workouts.

You could to this for example with a very light gripper (now your old plastic-handled gripper you could close for 500 reps finally come to use), or a foam or rubber ball, and light rubber bands for the hand extensors. Some tool with which you can perform at least 20 reps easily. Two to three sets of 10-20 reps per exercise and per hand should suffice.

2) Contrast baths

This is one of the most popular and effective ways to speed up hand recovery, and it was used by Tommy regularly. The idea is to alternately **expose your hands and forearms to very high and very low temperatures**, which really gets the blood circulation going (to an extent that the increased amount of blood in the areas will actually still be visible for a few minutes afterwards).

This is how you do it:
a) Take two five gallon buckets (as outlined in the equipment section, these should be part of your personal grip strength home gym).
b) Boil water on the stove to fill one of the buckets, but add some colder water to make sure you don't get burned. (Determining the right temperature for the hot water is rather tricky. If it's too hot, you get burned or won't be able to dip your hands into the bucket. If it's too cold you won't nearly have the recuperating effect you aim at. Experiment until you know how much cold water you need to add, etc. You may also want to use a thermometer to find out which temperature suits you, and to ensure the water has this exact temperature before you begin.)
c) Fill the other bucket with water as cold as possible, then add ice, as much as you can find. I developed the habit to reuse cottage cheese cans by filling them with water and freezing them, and always keeping two of them in my refrigerator (besides ice cubes)

for this purpose. (The resulting cylindrical chunks of ice are also perfect to play around with in your hands during the cold hand bath if you want this additional effect.)
d) Dip both hands into the hot water and keep them there for as long as you can bear.
e) Then immediately dip them in the cold water and do the same.
f) Repeat in the same manner for 10 minutes at least. IMPORTANT: Finish off with the cold water. After your last "bath" in the ice water bucket you should not put your hands into the hot water bucket again. Don't let me explain the reasons for this, as I don't know them myself. Just take my word for it that it is most effective this way.

There are two ways to do this. You can either keep your hands in the baths still, which has the effect that the hot water cools off more slowly, and vice versa with the cold water. Or you can move your hands around in the water, open and close them, wiggle your fingers around, stretch them, etc. to mobilize your muscles a bit. Try both and stick with whatever suits you best.

3) Mobilizing all muscles in your hands

Light training of the movements you usually perform in your workouts is only one side of the story. You should also do some exercises which mobilize **all the other small muscles in your hands and forearms**. It helps to release tension as well and maintains muscle balance by training all the muscles you do not reach in your heavy workouts. This is why "**finger walking**", as explained above in the Additional Training section can also be considered an excellent exercise for recovery.

Besides this exercise, Tommy recommends to use these little Chinese therapy balls, which mobilize your hand muscles by harmonic movements you don't normally perform in your grip strength workouts. He used them every single day in two variations, with palm up and palm down. Tommy also has a pair of six-pound shot puts he holds in his hands while rotating his wrists in each direction. He points out that these methods of active recovery seemed to help a lot. Give them a try.

4) Stretching

The opinions on the benefit of stretching for strength athletes are divided, but I firmly believe that stretching - if done correctly - has great health benefits and can be used effectively for recovery.[10] It has also been recommended to me independently by several physiotherapists after a grip

---

[10] Read the book *Relax Into Stretch* by Pavel Tsatsouline if you need to be convinced.

strength training-induced injury - to recover from said injury, but also to prevent future injuries. The main benefit for hand strength athletes in stretching lies in **relaxing your muscles and relieving tension** as part of your recovery program. To achieve this effect, you need to do it correctly. Observe the following guidelines:

a) Do not stretch directly before or after your grip strength workout, but, ideally, on a separate day.
b) When you stretch a muscle, go as far into the stretched positions that you feel the tension clearly, but not as far that you register pain.
c) Hold the stretched position for about 30 seconds at least, then release slowly.
d) For maximum effect, hold the stretched position for 30 seconds, then flex the muscles just being stretched hard and keep them flexed for 10 seconds. Then release tension again and aim to stretch a little bit further than before. Hold again for 30 seconds and release slowly.
e) Shake out your hands and wrists lightly afterwards.
f) Stretch your hands, fingers, and wrists in every conceivable direction. Here are some example positions:

Grip Strength

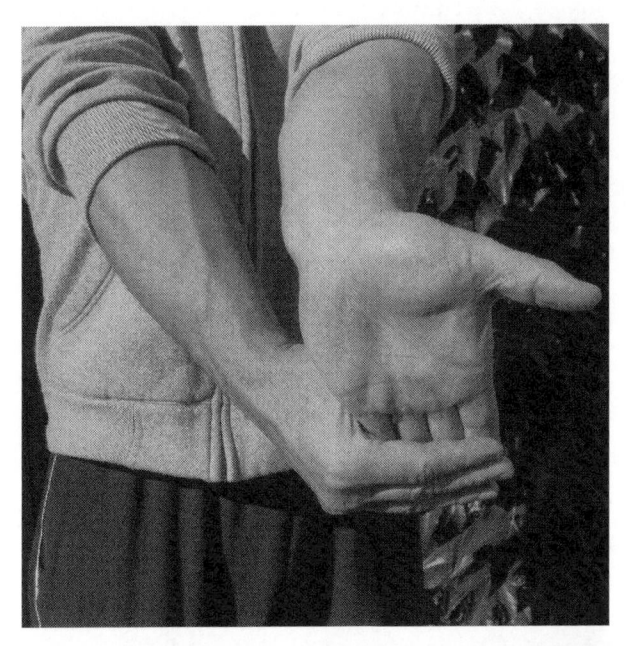

Robert Spindler with Tommy Heslep

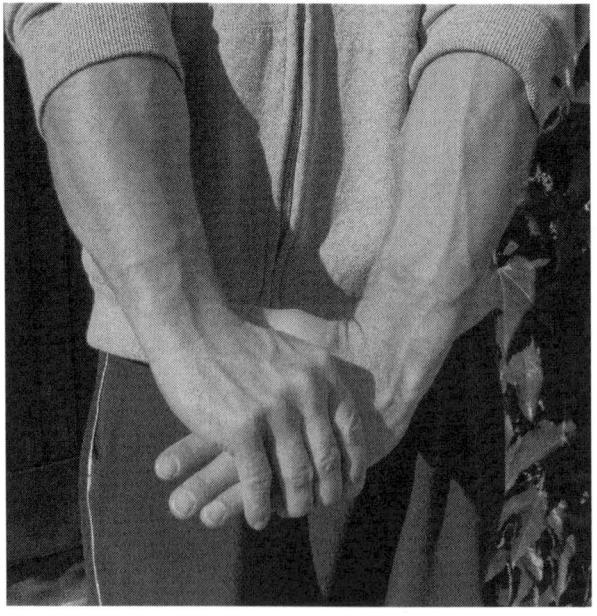

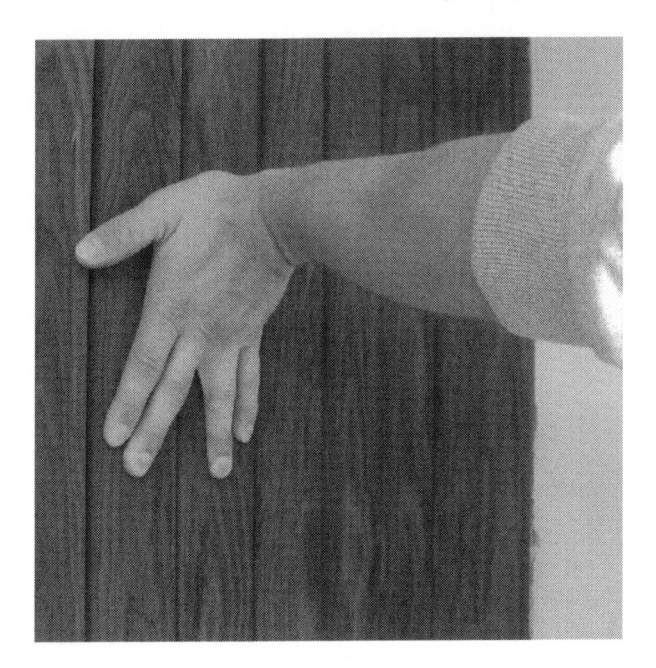

Fig. 11.1 Some sample stretching positions

One last word on stretching **before the workout**. A lot of people stretch before a workout as part of their warm-up program, which is absolutely fine. But: if you stretch to warm up, you should not hold the stretched positions statically for 30 seconds or whatever, but rather **stretch dynamically**, that is, go into a stretched position, but get out of it immediately and repeat this several times, let's say 10 times. In that way, stretching before the workout is a suitable warm-up exercise.

Stretching after your workout is, according to the present opinion of sport scientists, of no benefit.

For an optimum of recovery, combine any of these strategies - light workout, contrast baths, mobilizing of muscles, and stretching - into a half hour recovery session that suits you and go through it after a tough grip strength workout or on your rest days. (I wouldn't recommend contrast baths *before* a grip strength workout on the same day. I tried it once and the workout afterwards was lousy.) You may want to make such a recovery session a fixed part of your routine, let's say twice a week, or just resort to it when you feel the soreness in your hands after a workout which really taxed you. In any way, you will soon realize the positive effects of active and passive recovery, and probably not want to go without it any more. You can even go through such a recovery session while watching a DVD or television, as it won't distract you much. Take care of proper recovery yourself and you won't need dangerous drugs to do it for you. The fun will be all the same - if not more.

11.2. Plateaus

Let's say your goal is to close a certain gripper. Once you notice that you have reached a plateau and cannot make further gains towards your goal, one of three things is happening: Either 1) your **training impulses aren't intense enough** to stimulate further gains, or 2) you **aren't resting enough** to recuperate in between workouts, or 3) you have reached the natural **limit of your genetic potential**.

If you don't experience constant soreness in your hands (from lack of rest), and have not closed the #3 CoC® yet (the possible limit of your genetic potential), the problem is likely to be 1) - your training impulses are simply not intense enough. Then you should train with more intensity. But, at the same time, do a little less (in terms of sets, exercises or workout sessions per week), so the problem won't become 2), too little rest between workouts - else your gains will stagnate again. Tommy says, the more strain you put on your body, the more rest it needs so it can recuperate to do it again. Try some exercises you haven't tried yet, like strap holds - or get one of the "in between-grippers", like a #1.5, for new training impulses and greater intensity. But reduce the number of days you work out per week (if you train more than once a week) or the number of sets per exercise. Tommy recommends: "No marathon workouts - just get in and get out."

If this doesn't help to overcome the plateau, you may have entered problem phase 2) and your body may need a break. Tommy explains: "Depending on how long you've been trying, if you're really close to your goal and keep on trying and trying and trying for months, not getting anywhere, just take a break. A couple of weeks, perhaps. Don't pick them stupid little things up,[11] just let them lay there." He actually recommends, regardless of whether you reached a plateau or not, to take a week off every month or month and a half, simply to give your body a rest.

Don't worry too much that you have entered problem phase 3) as long as you are not absolutely sure whether more is possible. Tommy encourages you to not underestimate yourself, but at the same time he acknowledges that hard work is indispensable: "Keep doing the same thing and keep squeezing harder. Just don't give up. Keep your mind in the right place and don't quit, don't ever give up. Probably anybody off the street could close the Trainer, the #1, or the #2. Maybe even the #2.5. But to close the #3 and the #4 you

---

[11] He means the grippers.

definitely have to be more dedicated. It takes a different mind-set to do something that difficult. But I think it's possible. I know it's possible, because I did it. And I only weigh 158 pounds!"

> **Hint:**
>
> **While some like to test progress on their challenge gripper every week, this can drive others crazy, especially if the progress is hardly perceptible. For a change, try testing the challenge gripper only every four weeks or so. Don't even pick it up in the meantime! If you have trained vigorously with your working gripper, or with machines, you will notice substantial progress the next time you test the challenge gripper.**

11.3. Injury Prevention

The reasons for training injuries are manifold, and *anyone* I know who plays *any* sport with a level of intensity had to deal with injuries at one point in time, including Tommy and me. But this does not not mean that many of the common injuries can be prevented by following certain guidelines. I believe some of the more frequent reasons for training injuries in the context of strength training (which, other than most field sports, usually doesn't involve fast movements) are: a) attempting too fast progression, b) intense stress from unnatural angles and unusual motions, c) muscle imbalance, d) too sudden stress, e) lack of recovery.

In practice, you can avoid a) and b) by slow progression - increasing weights step by step - and always keeping an eye on proper technique. Now, in grip strength training, proper technique isn't that much of an issue as in deadlifts, squats, or power cleans, for example. There is not that much you can do wrong. Still, whenever you try a new exercise which stresses your muscles from an angle you aren't used to yet, **begin by using a light weight** until you and your body get used to the movement. I know this is boring, I know this sounds like a beginner's course, and I know light weights are for sissies. But training wisely is manly, and I will tell you why below.

We have talked about c), muscle imbalance, before. I believe the least of all hobby-athletes are aware that this can become a problem. Whenever you train a specific movement with intensity, you should **also train the opposing movement**. The same is true with left/right symmetry. Of course, everyone has his stronger side - for most right-handers this will be the right side - and they will aim to close their challenge gripper with this hand first. Still, your left side has the same "right to might" as your right side. So treat all parts of your body the same. Muscle imbalance can lead to slow, creeping problems that announce themselves before they are really there. Once they are there, they are all the harder to get rid off. And then, most of the time, you won't even know where they came from and misinterpret them. Such problems can be tenseness in your muscles, joint pains, back pain, bad posture, etc.

I've heard so many powerlifters say they don't train their abdominal muscles because "heavy squats and deadlifts stress them sufficiently." True, squats and deadlifts also stress your abdominal muscles, but the truth is, they stress your lower back muscles to a disproportionately higher degree. The consequence of too strong back muscles and too weak abdominal muscles, is then often - paradoxically, it seems - back problems, amounting to spinal disc damage. Who would think he could have prevented lower back pains by training his abs?[12] The same is true for the muscles in your forearm. You have

---

[12] Obviously, this is only one of the many triggers for damaged discs. If you have problems in this area, consult a doctor first before you attempt to cure yourself.

pains in your hands, wrists or forearms, and will think you overdid your grip strength training - when all you would have needed to do was to train your extensors as well.

Remember: this isn't a detail. It's essential. If you train the movement of closing your hand, also train the movement of opening your hand with rubber bands. This sums it up for most grip strength athletes.

Too avoid problem d), too sudden stress, always warm up. It's as simple as that. Follow the suggested warm up routine for gripper training: ten reps with a very light gripper, then ten reps with the next gripper, and so forth, to make sure you are properly warmed up before you touch your working or challenge gripper. It happens so often in my gym that when I take the CoC® Grippers out of my bag, someone comes along and wants to try one of them. I usually attempt to instruct them, but they leave you little time - they just grab a gripper and give it all they got to close it. I would never do this - even with a gripper I know I can close with medium effort. I **never touch a tougher gripper without specific warm-up**, because I know it has the potential to throw me back on my path. Even if someone challenges me. Let him call me sissy - I don't care. When my time comes - that is, when I'm doing my grip strength workout after a proper warm-up, I will refuse no challenge. Until then - in bars, at parties, whatever - I simply decline. Most of these challenges are stupid, anyway.

If you have just seen a video on YouTube with some crazy new grip strength feat, don't go right ahead and try it. Try it when you are ready. After a proper warm-up.

The fifth and last major reason for injuries, e) lack of recovery, is closely connected to a), attempting too fast progression, and b), intense stress from unnatural angles and unusual motions. If you train too often per week, for example, the specific muscles you use may not have fully recuperated, and you will use other muscles to compensate. These other muscles are perhaps not used to the new movement and you will get hurt.

In any case, treat the recovery process between workouts with the same respect as you treat the workouts themselves. Remember that **a few days of rest** may be the best thing you can do to your grip strength progress. Listen to your body's signals. If you hands are still sore from the workout the day before, consider a contrast bath for them. If you train your grip twice per week and don't make any progress, consider cutting back to once per week.

In sum, to prevent injuries, observe the following rules:

- do not attempt too fast progress
- feel your way towards any new and unusual movement cautiously
- train all opposing muscle groups in your hands and forearms equally
- always warm up in advance of intense stress on your muscles
- make recovery in between workouts a high priority

As I said before, injuries happen to anybody who plays a sport with intensity above average, so when it happens to you, go see a doctor.

If you need to fill in time until you can see one and the pain is acute, you might want to try the following for relief:

- take a chunk of ice or some ice cubes and wrap them up in a thin cloth
- cool the injured area for 7-10 minutes with it
- Take a 20 minute break during which you put the ice back into the freezing compartment
- cool the area again for 7-10 minutes (ice again wrapped in cloth)
- repeat 2-3 times a day

This will help to relief pain from many injuries and speed up the recovery process, but it might not be the best thing to do for ALL injuries. If you have the feeling it doesn't help, stop the cycle immediately and go see that doctor as soon as possible. Also, this cycle works best immediately after the injury happened. If you are in pain since five weeks already, don't cool the area with ice, as it might make things worse. And did I tell you to go see a doctor in any case?

Why it is manly to avoid injuries and treat them if they happen: Many men, especially the young ones, go into their training with the attitude: "no pain, no gain." Now, I prefer this attitude to the wimpy "my-training-may-be-useless-but-at-least-it doesn't-hurt-me" mindset some others seem to have when they enter the gym. Because the first group of men is much more likely to make fast progress. It's a fact that effective training involves an amount of pain.

But pain is relative, and it is necessary to differentiate between good and bad pain. Young trainees may think they are indestructible and keep on training regardless, even with creeping injuries (bad pain). I used to be one of them. But now I curb my enthusiasm with the following psychological trick: **the cave-man attitude.**

In the stone-age, men were dependent on their bodies to survive. Of what use is an injured cave-man to his tribe? Of little use - he cannot hunt, he cannot fight off enemies or beasts, he may not even be able to gather berries and roots. And back in those times you couldn't go to a doctor and take a few days off from work. This is why I tell myself that a cave-man would take good care not to get injured. And if he would get injured, he would take care to recover as fast as possible. Because any day he is unable to "work" could mean his and his tribe's end.

Cave-men needed to be tough, and many situations in their daily life required death-defying recklessness. But only to protect and nourish the weaker members of their tribe, not for personal amusement. I believe that whenever possible, a cave-men would avoid injuries, and treat them seriously if they happened. And, considering that he would do so for the benefit of not only himself but also of his family and tribe, I believe this is a very manly disposition - and there is no weakness in avoiding injuries. So don't try to be tougher than you should be.

> **Hint:**
> **To prevent the skin of your hands from tearing, you might want to consider using an oil-based hand cream regularly to keep your hands smooth. Especially when you spend a lot of time in the cold or wash your hands often.**

Summary

- As your muscles grow while they rest - not during training - recovery from heavy workouts is essential. A lack of recovery can lead to plateaus, and too much intensity to overcome a plateau can lead to injuries.
- Some effective methods to speed up the recovery process between grip strength workouts are: light training, contrast baths, training all the smaller muscles in your hand, and stretching.
- Pamper your hands with a recovery session consisting of any of the above once or twice a week or whenever your hands are unusually sore.
- There are three major reasons for reaching plateaus: too weak training impulses, too little rest between workouts, and limited genetic potential. The first two can be avoided.
- To prevent injuries, mind the following risks: attempting too fast progression, intense stress from unnatural angles and unusual motions, muscle imbalance, too sudden stress, and lack of recovery.
- Once injured, go see a doctor as soon as possible. For temporary relief you can try to cool the injured area with ice.

12. NUTRITION

In this chapter we will give you some basic advice on how to optimize your nutrition for maximum grip strength gains.

Obviously, there is no need to eat like a professional bodybuilder or sumo wrestler if you want to make great grip strength gains. Some of you might not even need to change their nutrition at all and will still make great progress. As you will not increase considerably in size once you begin with a serious grip strength routine (sorry about that), there is not much need to increase calorie or protein intake to supreme levels. However, it can never hurt to adjust your nutrition to that of an athlete if you have failed to do so previously. At least for the benefit of a better health.

While there is no need to follow the nutrition plan of a professional heavyweight bodybuilder, Tommy does recommend to watch your **protein intake**. Protein is the primary substance your body requires to repair your muscles after a strenuous workout. Tommy eats five or six meals a day and at least 30gr of protein per meal. Any kind of athletic activity which builds strength and muscles can benefit from an increased protein intake, so why should grip strength training be the exception? For convenience, you can use a quality protein powder. Most of the time Tommy would drink a protein shake after his grip strength workouts (which was all he would do in terms of a special pre- or post-workout meal). However, there is absolutely no need to consume a protein powder at all costs. You can optimize your nutrition perfectly with all-natural protein sources as well.

Tommy also believes that certain supplements help to keep your tendons and ligaments healthy, and speed up the recovery process. He recommends vitamins (especially vitamin C), minerals, and glucosamine. If you fear you have a shortage of either, or your tendons and ligaments routinely don't recover fast enough after workouts, you might want to try a quality vitamin/mineral supplement and glucosamine. It might be added that Tommy did not use any of these when he started out - but he acknowledges the advantages now. Remember that supplements are, as the name says, meant to *supplement* your nutrition, not to constitute it. They are no replacement for a regular, balanced diet.

Tommy's most important advice, however, is to **eat healthy and natural in general**, and to avoid processed ingredients. He himself used to eat a lot of junk routinely - until the day he was diagnosed with Chron's disease a few years ago. The sickness made him lose 25 pounds and he was almost certain it would kill him. Eventually though, and thanks to God, he "got a grip on it" and beat the sickness. One step in doing so was starting to eat healthy, raw organic food, and nothing processed. And now he swears on this lifestyle.

I'd like to support this view. Eating naturally will not only boost your athletic achievements, but will generally make you feel better and increase your health. A pleasant side-effect is that it protects our environment. Personally, I am a huge fan of Paleo-type diets (as described by Loren Cordain in *The Paleo Diet*, Robb Wolf in *The Paleo Solution*, or - my favourite - Mark Sisson in *The Primal Blueprint*), which emphasize animal protein, healthy fats, and lots of vegetables. I understand that many oppose the large amounts of animal protein in the Paleo-type diets for ethical reasons, but as they also stress the importance of eating organic, local, and seasonal foods, and animal products from humane keeping methods, you might want to give it a try and actually do something good. I believe the Paleo-type diets are the best diets around at the moment, health-wise.

Talking about health: Tommy points out that one advantage of grip strength training is that "you don't have to do what bodybuilders do to become the best. You can do it with gift and determination." No need for 8.000 calories a day, desperate diets, and dangerous dehydration. Just hard work, iron will, and a little bit of potential.

And **no drugs**. Tommy has heard people talking about steroids and hand strength and they said it didn't really help. He himself has no idea, actually, as he has never tried them (same for me). He has been accused, of course, which he finds quite funny: "Guys on steroids are huge, aggressive, and have acne all over their body. Have you looked at me? See how small I am? I wouldn't even know where to get them... People dying just to get bigger and stronger? No thank you. It ain't worth it." So if you think you have to be on drugs to make progress with your grip strength, think again. Tommy didn't need them - not even to close the IronMind® #4 Captains of Crush® Gripper - and most of the leading grip strength athletes around the world don't need them either (so they claim - but you have every reason to believe them).

Summary

- If you do any kind of strength training, the most important aspect of your nutrition is your protein intake, and grip strength training is no exception. Keep your protein intake high.
- When it comes to supplements, a protein powder makes sense if you have difficulties to ensure sufficient protein intake without one. It is no must, however. Vitamins (especially vitamin C), minerals, and glucosamine can help to keep your tendons and ligaments fit.
- Eating exclusively healthy and natural organic food is the best you can do to your body, and your grip strength endeavours will benefit as well. Avoid processed ingredients.
- We strongly recommend to keep away from performance-enhancing drugs. Not only may the side effects damage your health and the fact that you are a "drugger" diminish your accomplishments, but you can reach almost any goal in the grip strength game without drugs - as Tommy has proven.

13. COMMON MISTAKES
Most of the following seven mistakes should be clear by now, but let us sum them up again.

1) Lack of intensity
To be effective, a grip strength workout needs to be intense. Meaning it should be **so intense that...**
...you will need a specific warm-up.
...you should not be able to make more than ca. 10 reps of a specific dynamic exercise (exception: endurance strength training).
...you should not be able to hold any isometric exercises (e.g. holds) for longer than ca. 10 seconds (exception: endurance strength training).
...you should not be able to train a specific movement more often than twice a week.
...you should still feel the strain of a workout the day after.
...you should perform a negative rep as if you would hang on for life.
...it will require your full concentration.
...etc.

Many make the **mistake** that their grip workout is so light that they could repeat it any time and place without warm-up and with all kinds of distractions. Try to develop a conscience for intensity by asking yourself after each set: did I give it my all or could I have done more? Could I have held this for a second longer? Could I have done one more rep? Could I have done this with one pound more weight? If you do this in your next couple of workouts, you will soon realize: you have probably been economic in most of your grip strength workouts until now. In future, give it your all.

2) No systematic training
Have you wondered lately why your grip strength progress stagnates?

If your answer is yes, then try to answer the following questions for yourself: Has your grip strength training in the past consisted of more than a few fast reps squeezed out of a gripper during the last two minutes of your upper-body workout? Do you know the weaknesses and strengths of your grip? Do you perform specific exercises to tackle your weaknesses? Do you have all the equipment you need at hand? Do you have an action plan? Do you know when to train which aspect of your grip and with what exercises? Do you have a goal? Do you have a tactic to reach that goal? If yes, are you sure it works? Do you have a plan B if it doesn't work? Do you know when a break from training is due?

If your answer to more than one of these questions was no, your grip strength training could benefit if it was **more systematic**. Remember the third of Benjamin Franklin's thirteen virtues: "Order: Let all your things have their places, let each part of your business have its time." Apply this to your grip strength workout schedule - if you have one. And if you don't have one, get one already! Set yourself a goal and devise a plan to reach that goal. Leave enough time to concentrate on a proper grip strength session if you train other body parts as well. Know with which exercise to start and which exercise comes next and why. Focus on your weaknesses. Get organized. Have a system!

3) Lack of progress

Whether you have a system or not, your focus should always be on progress. Many make the mistake that they always do the same and maintain a certain level of strength, but progress stagnates and they wonder why. Or they don't wonder why, which is even worse. Such people probably believe that progress simply takes time. This is true, but at the same time progress has to be forced. It doesn't come by itself. You should **always aim for progress**: make one rep more than in the last workout, hang on for a second longer than last time, use one pound more weight. Even if you are unable to do this one additional rep, you should at least try. And if it doesn't happen within a considerable time-frame, change your strategy. Try a new exercise. Try negatives, try beyond the range training. Train more often or less often. Squeeze harder! But always aim for that next step and never be satisfied with were you stand (well, once you have closed the CoC® #4 you can be satisfied). Work on it.

Tommy acknowledges that keeping track of your progress helps, although he himself never kept track. He says sometimes he wishes he would have, but as you know Tommy was always bound to get ahead and never had a problem with motivation. If making progress is a problem for you, **keep track of the reps you make and the weight you use**, as well as the seconds you hold a specific static exercise. And try to beat that number in each consecutive workout. If progress stagnates, review your workout schedule and make some significant changes. If your hands feel constantly sore you might want to take a break as well. Then follow that new schedule and see what happens. If it works, keep at it, if it doesn't, try something else. But never leave your progress to chance. Because once you have reached a certain level of strength, further progress won't come by itself. It will require hard work.

Many perform their workout regularly and rigidly, but lose sight of progress. Don't make that mistake.

4) Doing too much

As much as some people's workouts lack intensity, as much can it be too intense. The most common mistake is probably to train **too often per**

week. Even the best grip strength athletes in the world don't train a specific grip strength aspect more often than twice a week, so why should you?

Also, an infinite number of sets are no automatic benefit. Think about it: Do you think that you will be able to perform each and every one of 30 sets with the same intensity as the first three? Only very few elite grip strength athletes can do that. Stick to the suggested number of reps, sets, and number of workouts per week suggested in this book and learn to focus your energy on the moment. Although you will have the feeling that you will train your grip rather little, with a low number of sets, train it with full intensity *when* you do and you will be fine.

If you are as enthusiastic about grip strength training as we, believe me, I know the problem: you can't wait to make progress, you can't wait to work on it, you can't wait to train. If you feel this way today but it's still three days until your next grip strength workout, do something else for your hands: train your extensors, have a light recovery workout, have a contrast bath for your hands. Visualize your workout in three days' time. Analyse your last grip strength workout and think about what you could do better. Make some notes. Then, when the time comes for your next workout session, approach it fully prepared. The benefit will be yours.

Doing too much can also mean doing little (with great intensity) over a too long period of time. Remember to **give your body a longer break every once in a while.** If you don't do this, you will probably learn it by yourself the hard way: If you follow an intense grip strength program month after month, year after year, you will probably realize at one point that you are moving in no direction at all. Now you run the risk that frustration spoils your fun in grip strength training forever. Beware: once you reach the point where you are not looking forward to your grip strength session this week at all, your body is probably sending you a signal that he needs a break. Then the time has definitely come to take a couple of weeks off - until you can't wait to get at it again.

5) Lack of balance

We said this several times before, but let us repeat it once more, as it is so important: you should train all parts of your hand equally. Tommy says: "Work the whole hands all the way round. Don't just use the grippers, but also focus of the extensors, the opening of the hand. And do finger walking. Don't neglect that - it really helps. And don't neglect your thumb either. It's part of the hand. Again: don't just do the grippers. Do everything all the way round."

So, if you train intensely with grippers - and we assume most of you who read this will - train at least **one other kind of grip strength which**

involves the thumb, like thick bar-lifting or pinch-lifting. Preferably, you try every grip exercise you can come up with every once in a while. And train your extensors with rubber bands. Wrap them around your fingertips, right at the fingernails, and open your hand against the resistance as wide as you can. Tommy still does this just about every other day. And he wishes he would have done it when he was going after the #4 CoC®. If he had, he probably wouldn't have messed up the tendon in his middle finger. So learn from his mistakes before you repeat them.

"Without balance, you're gonna get hurt," Tommy sums it up.

6) Wrong goal setting

Don't set your goals too low. Tommy thinks there is nothing wrong with setting goals that other people or even you think are impossible to achieve. He says: "Keep working on it and you'll achieve it. I did." Many guys will think that pinching two 45 lbs plates in one hand, deadlifting the Inch dumbbell, or closing a CoC® #3 is out of their reach. Those are the people who are satisfied with pinching two 35s, lifting the Baby Inch dumbbell, or closing the CoC® #2 and don't even try to achieve more. Truth is, a naturally strong friend of mine recently closed the CoC® #2.5 right away without doing any grip strength training beforehand at all. So don't believe you have achieved anything unusual if you do the same, and don't stop training. **There is always another goal**. Sure, you might not reach it, but trying and failing is better than not having tried at all, right? It's probably best to set yourself a goal which is one step beyond your actual next goal. If you want to close the #3, set yourself the goal of closing the #3.5. You might not be able to close the #3.5 in the end, but on your way to it, you will perhaps close the #3. Aim high and you will get somewhere at least. Aim low and you will get nowhere.

At the same time, stay realistic with your goals. If you can barely close the #1.5, it is not realistic that you will close the CoC® #4 within six months. Remember that Tommy got the #3 in 1998 and got certified for it in 2001 (three years later). He got certified for the #4 in 2004 (again three years later). It takes time to grow and it takes time to build world-class grip strength as well. Perhaps, if you have perfect conditions, you will be faster. But don't start out by lying to yourself. Calculate with a realistic time-frame to reach your goal and take one step at a time. You may aim high, but aiming too high is foolish. Perseverance is the key.

Having realized that it takes time to reach your goals, try not to lose sight of them. And don't get discouraged. "Don't let anything negative get in your way," Tommy says. "Always be positive. I always be positive, cause my blood type is B positive. I can't be negative. It's impossible."

7) Not taking advice or taking the wrong advice

Sometimes it is amazing how easily new trainees can be manipulated. A member of some cheesy bodybuilding forum may tell them in eloquent speech exactly what they need to do to make progress and they will blindly follow his advice without ever having met the guy in person, without being sure that he actually is the person on his profile pictures, and without being sure the achievements listed in his profile aren't lies.

On the other hand are those trainees who believe they found a revolutionary training system on their own, and they just need to stick to it to grow big and strong faster than anybody else. If an expert in strength training tries to give one of those a well-meant piece of advice, all the trainee will think to himself is, "Ha ha, you just wait and see, with my kind of system I will be stronger than you in a few weeks' time."

Be neither of both. Always seek advice, but **seek valuable advice and seek it in the right place**. Here are some criteria of valuable strength training advice, to help you separate the wheat from the chaff. Trustworthy training advice...:

- ...is conservative
- ...is logic
- ...is time-tested
- ...emphasises hard work and intensity
- ...is kept simple
- ...emphasises perseverance
- ...doesn't involve great secondary costs

You should be extra cautious with advice which...:

- ...is advertised as "revolutionary", "brand new", "the latest" or similar adjectives
- ...lacks transparency
- ...has never been heard of before
- ...promises results with little effort
- ...sounds utterly complicated
- ...promises results in no time
- ...requires loads of expensive equipment to be followed

If you are taking advice from a person, check whether he...:

- ...has himself achieved what you are trying to achieve
- ...has done so without the help of drugs
- ...has been in the game for a considerable amount of years
- ...isn't a complete moron

- ...doesn't make an additional financial profit if you follow his advice

Don't get the last point wrong: the best advice is never free. If you have to pay for it, it is actually a good indication that a piece of advice is "valuable". But once you have paid money for a book, DVD, etc. and it tells you that you have to buy this and that product (coming from the same person) as well in order to make gains, you should reconsider whether you have picked the right advisor.

I like to compare strength training to stock picking: you will always have people coming along with tips and strategies for massive profits within a short period of time. You may follow their advice and hope to win, but you also run the risk that their advice is trash and you will lose. The better strategy is usually a conservative one, which promises moderate profits over a longer period of time. In the long run, you will always win with such a strategy. And, as people like Benjamin Graham, David Dodd, and Warren Buffett have demonstrated, an intelligent, timeless, and largely conservative strategy brings the greatest profits in the long run.

At the end of this book you will find a list with books and DVDs which fulfil the criteria for valuable training advice, have stood the test of time, and come from people who know what they are talking about. When Tommy started out, there wasn't much info on grip strength training out there and he pretty much taught everything himself. Luckily, a couple of sources for valuable grip strength training advice are available these days. Take advantage of them.

One last word on following advice though: While you shouldn't believe you don't need any advice at all, and while you shouldn't follow the wrong advice blindly, remember not to follow "quality" advice blindly either. Ultimately, you must find out what works for you, and nobody can tell you *exactly* what this is, because everybody is different. You should definitely try what worked for those who have achieved greatness in the grip strength game. But even if it worked for them, it may not work for you. Then you should try something else. Ultimately, you must be able to adapt.

Summary
- Make sure that your grip strength training doesn't lack the necessary intensity.
- Make sure your grip strength training is systematic so that you know what to train when, how and why.
- You should always focus on progress. Never be satisfied with where you are. If progress stagnates, change something in your training.
- If you belong to the over-motivated type of trainee, check whether you are not doing too much. Training a specific grip strength aspect more often than twice a week with intensity may be counterproductive.
- Watch for balance and always train all aspects of grip strength, or as many as you can think of. Don't neglect the hand extensors, the thumb, and the small muscles in the hand which can be trained with finger walking.
- Set yourself realistic goals, but don't be afraid to aim high.
- Be careful which advice you follow and prefer conservative training advice over promises of a revolutionary program.

14. AFTERWORD

Now that you have learned about the world's best methods to maximize your grip strength potential, you might feel a bit overwhelmed: I need to have my own grip strength gym? I have train my grip from dozens of angles, several times a week? I have to buy equipment worth hundreds of dollars?

If you want a world-class grip, the answer is yes, yes, and almost (you can save a lot of money with the advice in this book). But there is absolutely no reason why you shouldn't go step by step. Start with a heavy duty gripper from the cheapest company, two wooden blocks, and a bucket of rice - once a week. See how it feels. If you can get anywhere you want to with those, fine. However, if it's fun and you want more, stack up on equipment and effort and see where it leads you. Who knows, maybe you will be the next one who certifies for one of the heavy duty grippers?

In any case, I want you to remember the basics you learned about in this book: the different types of hand strength, why you should train all of them if possible, how to train them for maximum results, and how to avoid and treat injuries the best way you can. Keep those in mind and pick from the rest whatever you need for your specific goals and purposes. Just never lose sight of why you started grip strength training and keep at it. We are confident that you will make substantial progress in due time.

I always felt that grip strength is something special. It is more than a sport you play for some time and then give up to try something else. A strong grip is a personality trait and a lifetime achievement. And we hope you will enjoy the benefits of strong, healthy hands and the respect a powerful grip commands for the rest of your life.

We wish you all the best with your training.

RECOMMENDED BOOKS AND DVDS

- Get a Grip with Joe Kinney: Special Edition (DVD)

(This handsome DVD contains a home-made video training guide by Joe Kinney, the first man who closed the #4 gripper, and a more recent two-hour interview with Joe conducted by John Wood. In contains equipment demonstrations and a truly inspiring clip of Joe closing the #4. Available on functionalhandstrength.com.)

- Randall J. Strossen, J.B. Kinney, and Nathan Holle, The Captains of Crush® Grippers: What they are and How to Close Them.

(This book traces the history of the Captains of Crush® Grippers in detail for those who are interested. It also contains two chapters by the first two men who closed the #4 gripper, Joe Kinney and Nathan Holle, explaining their training. Kinney's chapter is quite complete and also a bit philosophical; a great read. Available on ironmind.com or amazon.com, also as a Kindle ebook.)

- John Brookfield, Mastery of Hand Strength and The Grip Master's Manual.

(Two modern-day classics. Tommy learned a lot from the first book by grip strength pioneer John Brookfield, and so did a lot of other people. Tommy especially liked the home-made equipment Brookfield presents in there. The second book is supposed to "start where Mastery of Hand Strength" *stops, but many of the things in the first book you will also find in the second one, plus a lot more. Both highly recommended and available on ironmind.com or amazon.com, also as a Kindle ebook.)*

- Brooks Kubik, Dinosaur Training - Lost Secrets of Strength and Development.

(Brooks Kubik's classic Dinosaur Training *is about the most motivating book I've ever read, and although he writes about strength training in general, he puts great emphasis on grip strength training, especially with thick bars. His attitude towards high-intensity, old-school, and drug-free training is exemplary.)*

- Jedd Johnson, Card Tearing E-book, Crush! DVD, etc.

(Jedd Johnson made the effort to put together a whole E-Book on how to tear decks of cards. Available at cardtearing.com. His DVD Program Crush! *focuses on the closing of heavy grippers. It is available on dieselcrew.com, together with his other useful products.)*

DID YOU LIKE THIS BOOK?

Whether yes or no, you can do me a big favour:

Write me a short e-mail saying what you liked or didn't like about the book at

robert.spindler@gmail.com

Just give me a short feedback.

I'm trying to improve my products constantly to help my readers become strong and stay healthy the best way possible.

Thank you.

For regular news and updates, join me at:

www.facebook.com/robert.eisenhans.spindler

Printed in Great Britain
by Amazon